PASTOR ABUSERS

WHEN SHEEP ATTACK

THEIR SHEPHERD

Kent Crockett

Pastor Abusers
Kent Crockett
125 E. Poplar St.
Prattville, Alabama 36066

Copyright ©2012 Kent Crockett

All rights reserved. No part of this publication may be reproduced, stored in a retrieval system, or transmitted in any form or by any means—printed, written, electronic, mechanical, photocopied, recorded, or otherwise—except for brief quotations, without the prior permission from the authors.

Except where otherwise indicated, Scripture quotations in this book are taken from the New American Standard Bible®, ©1960, 1962, 1963, 1968, 1971, 1972, 1973, 1975, 1977, 1995 by The Lockman Foundation. Used by permission. (www.Lockman.org)

Scripture quotations marked (CEV) are from the Contemporary English Version Copyright © 1991, 1992, 1995 by American Bible Society, Used by Permission.

Scripture quotations marked (NLT) are taken from the Holy Bible, New Living Translation, copyright © 1996, 2004. Used by permission of Tyndale House Publishers, Inc., Wheaton, Illinois 60189. All rights reserved.

Scripture quotations marked (NKJV) are taken from the New King James Version. Copyright © 1982 by Thomas Nelson, Inc. Used by permission. All rights reserved.

Italics in Scripture have been added by the author for emphasis.

Cover design by Chris Tripputi, Element City Graphics

ISBN 978-1-4675-3294-5

CONTACT INFORMATION
kent@kentcrockett.com

BIBLE STUDIES AND RESOURCES
www.kentcrockett.blogspot.com
www.makinglifecount.net

Dedication

To all pastors and ministers of the gospel who have been persecuted for the sake of righteousness.

"They will make you outcasts from the synagogue, but an hour is coming for everyone who kills you to think that he is offering service to God."
(John 16:2)

Acknowledgments

My thanks to the following:

Mike Johnston, who added much wisdom and insight to this manuscript. This book would not have been possible without you.

My wife, who has faithfully supported me through years of challenging ministry.

To the abused pastors who were willing to share their stories with us in order to help other ministers learn from their experiences.

Pastor Max Wilkins and the elders of The Family Church, Gainesville, Florida, for being examples of godly leadership.

Jack and April Sameck, Margaret Applegate, and Debbie Cenatiempo for your prayers and support in making this book a reality.

Contents

Preface	A Word from the Author	6
Chapter 1	The Secret Church Scandal	8
Chapter 2	Satan's Strategy to Expel the Pastor	21
Chapter 3	The Driving Forces Behind Pastor Abuse	36
Chapter 4	Signs of Impending Trouble	55
Chapter 5	You Might Be a Pastor Abuser If...	68
Chapter 6	The Silent Majority	82
Chapter 7	Do Demons Attend Church?	95
Chapter 8	Submission is not a Curse Word	105
Chapter 9	Closing the Loophole	118
Chapter 10	21 Things You Can Do Right Now	130
Chapter 11	Showdown with the Abusers	149
Chapter 12	Life After Leaving: What Do I Do Now?	159

Appendix

A Pastor's Wife Speaks Out	176
The Fellowship of His Sufferings	179
Bad Resume	181
Good Resume	185
Internet Job Listings	187

A Word from the Author

If you are a pastor who is experiencing turmoil with members of your congregation, we recommend that you do everything in your power to resolve the dispute. If you and your adversaries are willing to work through your differences, many areas of disagreement can be settled.

Unfortunately, many people don't want reconciliation. Saul never wanted to make peace with David. A book on conflict resolution never would have helped Paul get along with those who were plotting to kill him. If you have already tried every effort to make peace, and those who oppose you won't reciprocate, you need a different set of instructions. This book is a *survival manual* to show you what to do.

An abused wife who has been beaten by her husband doesn't need more advice on what she can do to make him happy. She needs to know how to protect herself. A pastor who is being abused by members of his congregation also needs to know how to survive and protect his family.

The stories in this book are true. Dozens of abused pastors were interviewed and they will tell their stories in their own words. Their names have been changed but the testimonies are accurate. The pastors I interviewed represent a wide variety of denominations from different states in America, yet the details of how they were abused by church members were remarkably similar. Their disturbing quotes are included in every chapter.

Whenever I talked with an abused pastor, he typically gave me three or four more names of other ministers who had been unjustly fired or forced out of their churches. I collected far more names than I was able to interview.

I also sought to only interview ministers who were known to be men of integrity and above reproach. The harassment they received wasn't due to them being immoral, unethical, or cruel dictators. They were innocent shepherds who were maliciously persecuted by mean-spirited members of their own congregations. Many of them are no longer pastors but are now working secular jobs.

As you read these ministers' shocking testimonies, keep in mind that vast majority of church members are friendly people who support their pastor. In many churches, the people who attack the pastor comprise only a small percentage of the congregation. Although they are a minority, they are more powerful than the majority, making them a pastor's worst nightmare.

Can anything be done to stop them? How widespread is this problem? What can a pastor do when he is under attack? Why won't his supporters speak up for him? What are his options if he is fired or forced out of his church? All those questions will be answered in this book.

If you are a seminary student or in Bible college, please don't assume that every church is abusive and this will inevitably happen to you. Many churches are caring congregations where you can have years of successful ministry. Hopefully this book will help you identify and avoid those churches that have a track record of attacking their previous pastors.

My friend Pastor Mike Johnston was a tremendous help to me and I've included his stories and comments throughout the book. I hope that you will find strength and encouragement to continue ministering, realizing that you are not alone in suffering for the work of the Lord.

Kent Crockett

Chapter 1

The Secret Church Scandal

"Behold, I send you out as sheep in the midst of wolves; therefore be shrewd as serpents, and innocent as doves." (Matt. 10:16)

At age twenty-six, one of the most brilliant men in Colonial America, Jonathan Edwards, became pastor of a church in Northampton, Massachusetts. Five years later, he became a leading voice in what later came to be known as the Great Awakening. He was considered America's first and possibly greatest theologian. His powerful sermons and books stirred the colonies. Many thousands were converted to Christ during his ministry.

What you may not know about Jonathan Edwards is—his own church voted to fire him! Unbelievably, someone in his congregation spearheaded the termination of a man God was using to revive an entire nation. Edwards was left to care for his wife and ten children.[1]

We've all heard stories about abusive pastors; false shepherds who are despicable, domineering, and manipulative. They treat their congregations harshly. They might be having an affair, or misusing offerings for personal gain. These cruel, unrepentant pastors bring shame to the name of Jesus Christ and need to be held accountable for their actions.

But you probably haven't heard about a different kind of church scandal. Newspapers don't print stories about this injustice. Even most church people are ignorant about the disgrace taking place right under their noses. But ask any pastor who has served in two or three congregations and he can tell you more horror stories than you care to hear—if you can get him to talk about them.

The secret church scandal we're talking about is the persecution of the pastor by mean-spirited people within the church, who are the "pastor abusers." They're planted in nearly every congregation. Many

---

[1] Harbour, Brian. *Brian's Lines*, Vol. 5, No. 12, December 1989.

are even running the church. They may be deacons, disloyal staff members, or members of the congregation who are determined to destroy the pastor through personal attacks, slander, and criticism. Outwardly they may look respectable, but inwardly their hearts are wicked, and their mission is to bring down their spiritual leader.

If Satan can't get a pastor to fall into corruption and immorality, he resorts to Plan B—persecution. Just as Jonathan Edwards was fired nearly three centuries ago, multitudes of pastors today are unjustly driven out of their churches.

Pastor abuse is the church scandal that no one is talking about. The mistreatment of clergy is as horrifying as it is secretive, and the casualties are reaching epidemic proportions. Over 19,000 pastors get out of the ministry every year. When the sermon ends on Sunday, over 350 pastors will be gone before the next Sunday service begins.

But the saga doesn't end with an empty pulpit. After the abusive church has fired the pastor and washed their hands of guilt, they carry on business as usual. Yet, a more tragic story unfolds in the ousted pastor's household. The abrupt change in plans throws the ex-pastor and his family into a financial crisis, forcing them to sell their home and frantically search for a new place to move. Without a church income, he'll need to go find a secular job. A terminated pastor shared his feelings:

> They don't care what happens to you. They don't care what happens to your family. They don't care what happens to your children. When they fired me, they didn't care that I had to jerk my kids out of school just after they had gotten started for that year. They don't care—just so long as you're gone.

Few people can truly understand how emotionally devastating it is for a minister to be severed from his congregation. A sharp blade cuts deep into his heart, every time he reflects on being rejected by those he poured his life into. As one former pastor described it: "It's like going through a divorce with hundreds of people at once."

And church ministry can be just as harsh on the pastor's wife. The following testimony from an abused pastor explains how the mistreatment by a few antagonists affected his spouse:

> I wouldn't allow the small group of troublemakers in our church to bring me down, but it was more than I could take when my wife had

an emotional breakdown. As I held her in my arms, she cried uncontrollably, sobbing a few words at a time: "All we've tried to do . . . is love these people . . . and all we get in return . . . is *hate*."

This wasn't what I anticipated when I was preparing for ministry in seminary. No one warned me about psychopathic church members and how they would affect my family. I wasn't about to lose my wife over a church! She's the most godly and gentle servant of God that I know, and it ripped my heart apart to see my devastated wife in a crumpled heap.

By God's grace, the cruel people left our church and she recovered from her devastation. Everything was fine for the next few years, until two disgruntled members unleashed more vicious attacks. My wife had an even worse breakdown this time, crying every day and sometimes unable to stop.

That did it—we were done! I started looking for a new place to go, and the Lord mercifully opened a door for me to work in a Christian organization.

Her experience isn't an isolated case. Eighty percent of pastors' wives wish their husbands would choose another profession.[2] And don't think that their husbands haven't thought about it. Fifty percent of pastors are so discouraged they would leave the ministry immediately if they could make a living any other way.[3]

What is it about the ministry that's causing so many to leave? Simply stated, it's a hostile group within nearly every church that criticizes, harasses, and bullies their pastor until he's so beaten down and discouraged that getting out of the ministry looks better than staying in. It's the persecution of the pastor—not by atheists, but by mean-spirited people *inside* the church.

God's messengers have always been mistreated. The Old Testament prophets, New Testament apostles, and Jesus Himself all suffered for speaking the truth to unbending, religious people. Why do we assume that it won't happen to us today? In this book, we'll demonstrate how the harassment pastors are receiving from stubborn church members can be traced back to the mistreatment of the Old Testament prophets.

While some shepherds have been physically tortured for their faith, most pastors are persecuted through persistent verbal attacks, criticisms, false accusations, and malicious slander, which ultimately

---

[2] "Statistics About Pastors." Maranatha Life's Life-Line for Pastors.
[3] ibid.

lead to resignation or termination. When the abusers start unleashing their hostility, some pastors take this as a warning sign to get out while they can. They'll secretly mail their resumes to churches in need of a pastor, trying to secure a new place to go before they are either fired or forced to resign.

In many churches, the pastor is terminated unexpectedly, which usually leaves him without an income and nowhere to go. His dismissal also serves as a death sentence for any future ministry. Once he's been terminated, he is viewed as a leper by pastor search committees, who immediately reject resumes from fired clergy. As a result, the former pastor will probably be forced to switch careers, discard his seminary education, and search for secular employment.

The Minority Rules

As hard to believe as it is, the hostile group that forces a pastor out of the church is typically only seven to ten people, or just 3% to 4% of the congregation.[4] These confrontational individuals often call secret meetings to conspire against the pastor and plot his firing.

Unbelievably, seminaries and Bible schools fail to adequately prepare their students for the mistreatment they are about to experience from these tyrants. Although ministerial students are trained to care for cooperative church members, little is mentioned about how to handle antagonists in the flock. Consequently, when the abusers begin their onslaught, the pastor is caught off-guard, not knowing how to defend himself.

Although most church members support their minister, they passively allow aggressive egotists to take control the church and thus perpetuate the problem of clergy abuse. The typical pastor, weary of fighting troublemakers, ends his ministry career after fourteen years and then finds employment in the secular field.[5]

You would think that the church would be the safest place for a minister to raise his family, and it should be. But when uncooperative, headstrong laymen stubbornly resist the pastor's leadership, it brings untold misery into his household. Prepare to hold your breath as you read these horrifying statistics:

---

[4] LaRue, John C. "Forced Exits: High-Risk Churches." *Your Church,* May/June 1996.
[5] Barna, George. *1996 Index of Leading Spiritual Indicators.*

- 1,600 pastors leave the ministry each month.[6]
- 25% of current pastors have been terminated at some point in their career.[7]
- 33% of churches either fired their last pastor or forced him to leave.[8]
- 90% of pastors said the hardest thing about ministry is dealing with uncooperative people.
- 70% of pastors feel grossly underpaid.
- 80% of pastors say their ministry has had a negative impact on their children.[9]
- 65% of pastors have thought recently about giving up on ministry.[10]
- 80% of pastors' wives feel left out and unappreciated by the church members.
- Over 50% report a serious conflict with a church member at least once a month.[11]

This disturbing data represents what is happening to God's called and gifted servants—perhaps even to you. To demonstrate how widespread this crisis has become, one pastor shared this report:

> In one year, 27 ministers in my district were forced to resign their pastorates, without charges of wrongdoing, unethical behavior, or immorality. Many because they were causing growth. Most cases it was the power bloc that ran the church that had them removed. Many have lost their pastorates, many their reputations and many have lost their enthusiasm about staying in the ministry.

---

[6] Brown, Jim. "Groups Seeking Causes of Alarming Clergy Dropout Rate." Agape Press, March 2, 2001.
[7] LaRue. "Forced Exits: A Too-Common Ministry Hazard." *Your Church*, Mar/Apr 1996, 72.
[8] ibid.
[9] Cannistraci, David. "Your Pastor is Under Attack." *Charisma*, October 23, 2003.
[10] ibid.
[11] Murphy, Richard. "Bad News About Your Pastor." Maranatha Life. Unless cited otherwise, these statistics have been gleaned from various sources such as Pastor to Pastor, Focus on the Family, Ministries Today, Charisma Magazine, TNT Ministries, Campus Crusade for Christ and the Global Pastors Network. http://maranathalife.com/lifeline/bad-news.htm

Another pastor shares his observations concerning the alarming rate of minister attrition, and places much of the blame on angry, critical members of the congregation:

> As I reflect on 35 years of ministry, I realize that many of my former colleagues are no longer pastors. Somewhere along the line, they left their "calling" and undertook a different path for their lives. Reflecting on my friends who used to be pastors, I realize that they are now a majority. Those, like me, who have stayed in ministry are actually the minority. The attrition rate has been high and the cost to souls is astronomical.
>
> The majority of my acquaintances encountered such turmoil and situational conflict (from church members) that they felt they could not continue to pastor. Congregations overwhelmed my pastor friends with unrealistic expectations, negative criticism and misplaced anger. Some congregations even assumed the perfect pastor was "out there," so their fallible pastor was terminated.[12]

Abuse is No Excuse

No matter how bad a marriage may be, spousal abuse is inexcusable. "Wife abuse" occurs when cruel husbands attempt to beat their wives into submission or drive them away in divorce. It occurs in such normal looking settings you would hardly ever suspect it.

"Pastor abuse" is frighteningly similar to this. The pastor isn't physically beaten, but is so mentally tormented, emotionally stripped, and spiritually trampled on that it kills his desire to minister. Although the abuser can be one person, it typically occurs when a group of disgruntled church members band together to hammer their pastor into submission or drive him out of the church. Sometimes he'll submit to the abuse because he believes it's better to take the beatings than to be thrown out on the street. Because pastor abuse is generally instigated by a relatively small circle, most church members have no idea what's happening behind the scenes.

The Typical Pastor Abuse Scenario

The harassment can be administered in a variety of ways, but usually starts with innocently sounding suggestions of things the pastor might do differently. Most pastors are receptive to fresh ideas concerning

---

[12] "Why Are So Many Pastors Leaving the Ministry?" Focus on the Family.

how to improve the ministries of the church. When good suggestions are successfully implemented, everyone wins.

However, when a suggestion comes from clergy abusers, it usually pertains to an issue that contests the pastor's leadership. It's designed as a test to see if the minister will give way to a controlling, antagonistic group. At first, the shepherd may not realize these "suggestions" are actually orders coming from his adversaries, who have a hidden agenda. However, if he doesn't take the hint, he will be reminded again in a more ominous way.

The ringleader will probably ask the pastor to meet him for lunch—not for fellowship, but to get his undivided attention about an issue or complaint. After some light small talk, the spokesman explains his concerns and the steps for dealing with them.

If his intimidation proves to be fruitless, the thermostat is turned up. Even though most of the congregation supports him, the handful of unhappy members starts their campaign to change minds by sharing their "concerns" with others. They spread gossip with those who are most likely to advance their cause, trying to expand their sphere of influence. Without exception, tidbits of information are stretched, distorted, and magnified, as the case is built against the pastor.

The pastor senses something is going on behind the scenes. Some members who were previously friendly are now avoiding him. Those who used to warmly smile at him now wear scowls on their faces. He's puzzled by their change in behavior and wonders what he did to offend them.

By now he's received a few angry emails or notes of disagreement, criticizing him about a number of issues that he's not handling properly. Some of the notes are left unsigned, making his attackers undetectable so he can't respond to them. The criticisms against him escalate, and the conflict drags on for weeks. Every decision he makes is countered with a rebuttal from his persecutors. He receives phone calls in the middle of the night, where an unrecognizable voice tells him to get out of the church and then hangs up.

The ringleader calls a secret meeting, inviting only the disgruntled church members. The gripe session against the pastor quickly turns into a feeding frenzy, like sharks smelling blood. Before the evening ends, the angry dissenters join themselves together to drive the pastor out of the church.

As the minister wrestles with his competency and calling, the fog lifts and what was hidden before is now obvious. It dawns on him—

these pastor-attackers aren't showing any mercy, kindness, or compassion toward their God-called leader. They magnify his every inadequacy and twist the truth with phantom allegations, which puts a negative spin on every good work the pastor attempts to do. Rather than letting the shepherd lead, they apply more pressure so he will surrender to their demands.

The pastor finds himself tossing and turning at night. He can't eat, sleep, or concentrate. His wife is suffering even more, as she helplessly watches her loved one being destroyed right before her eyes. She worries that the anti-pastor faction will force her husband out and frets about the future of her family if he loses his job. His children wonder why he's been edgy lately, but he can't tell them, lest they turn their anger against God.

The joy he had when he first came to the church has been replaced with misery and anguish. Ironically, the very members who had previously extended the call are the ones trying to expel him. His focus shifts from reaching the lost and making disciples, to answering allegations and squashing rumors. His vision for growing the church has been crushed. Now the only vision he has is seeing the moving van in front of his home.

Another secret meeting is called to decide the strategy for ousting the pastor. The details are hashed out, the date is confirmed on the calendar, and the plan is ready to launch.

The final blow is generally administered in a meeting between the pastor and the confrontational group. The anti-pastor faction shows up in full-force, unleashing a barrage of vicious attacks and unwilling to accept any option other than termination. By now the pastor is so battered and worn out, all he can think about is leaving. With no more will to resist, he is either fired or forced to resign.

Once terminated, the pastor must make a gut-wrenching decision—either stay in the pastorate or get out. He asks himself, *Do I want to put my family through this again in another church? I've barely survived this ordeal, and I can't fathom the thought of going through it again.* The other option is to start a new career in a secular vocation, but where? What kind of job is looking to hire a fired preacher? Either way, it's going to be an extremely tough road ahead. (I'll provide some helpful guidance in another chapter.)

Meanwhile, the revolving door at the church makes another turn. As the fired pastor makes his exit, the old guard looks to find another pastor who will meet all of their expectations, and history repeats itself with a new victim. Just like the abusive husband beats his next wife, the abusive church will mistreat its next pastor. A former Church of Christ pastor gave us this account:

> I recently spent some time with the pastor who took my place, and he started pouring his heart out to me. He's only been there a few weeks and he's already being criticized for minor things. One person has already been complaining to others, "I think the new pastor has an agenda." I looked at him and jokingly said, "Let the beatings begin!"
>
> It's just being a part of being a pastor in America. They just want to use you as a punching bag. He asked me if I was ever going back to being a pastor. I told him, "I'm not doing that again. I'm not going to subject myself or my wife to that anymore—not to the way we do church in America nowadays. I would have to have a burning bush experience to know it was God telling me to do it again."

Incredibly, no matter how cruel a church may be, over two hundred eager (but foolish) pastoral candidates will submit their resumes to replace him, without researching the reasons for the former minister's departure.[13] If a prospect does his homework and gets suspicious, the pastor haters are crafty at manipulating their story and covering their tracks, so they come out smelling like a rose.

Why is this group so hostile toward its pastor? They want to be the church bosses and will resist anyone who attempts to lead them out of their comfort zones. The anti-pastor faction refuses to let the shepherd guide them and rejects all ideas that don't originate with them. When ungodly, unqualified individuals wield swords of authority in the church, pastor abuse is inevitable.

The pastor is constantly learning about the most effective ways to reach people through church growth conferences, pastor training workshops, and cutting-edge books. Then he hits a wall of resistance when he tries to implement these new ideas in his congregation. He unfortunately discovers the old guard bristles at ideas they didn't initiate. They're nervous about trying something they've never done before and prefer to keep the church as it's always been. These are two completely different mindsets, and only one can and ultimately will rule the church.

---

[13] Numerous churches were contacted that had advertised for a pastor. Every church had received anywhere from 200 to 350 resumes for the one vacant position.

Pastor Mike Johnston's Tragic Experience

I was never called to be a politician. I was called to preach the matchless grace of Jesus Christ. The Spirit of the Living God placed a burden on me that multitudes of lost and empty people desperately need Jesus. I knew exactly what Paul meant when he wrote, "woe unto me if I do not preach the gospel."

I remember being so excited about winning souls and building the church I could think of little else. In fact, I often quoted Hank Aaron who said, "I still can't believe they pay me to play baseball." I felt the same way about ministry.

In my naiveté, I believed that if I faithfully followed my calling with integrity, the sheep would naturally follow the shepherd. And while most of my flock did joyfully follow my lead, a small group of pastor-resisters were also sitting in the pews plotting my demise. Jesus warned us to beware of those who come in sheep's clothing but inwardly are ravenous wolves (Matt. 7:15). Whenever I read that verse, I always thought it applied to someone else. Little did I realize that they resided inside the church where God had called me, and I was on their menu.

If you have never experienced pastor abuse then you will probably not understand my next statement. *My heart may never be whole again!* Call me a crybaby or whatever you want. But please understand that trying to expunge memories of the misery they caused me and my family has been difficult, to say the least. You always loathe what happened to you because it is so personal, unjust and horrifying. Please forgive my candor, but I have only recently found the strength to pray God's blessing on my persecutors.

The conflict began a year and a half after I accepted the call to the church and lasted for two grueling years. The church was in a spirit of revival and we were growing dramatically. Yet, as I preached, I noticed that some members' icy stares penetrated my soul like cold, steel daggers. It became clear to me that these people were angry about the influx of all the new members. God had been blessing our services in every way imaginable and they were losing control!

This wasn't the first time they had intimidated their pastor and it wouldn't be their last. My predecessor had been fired and the pastor who followed me was also terminated just one year after he was hired. Despite the old guard's reputation as pastor abusers, I thought they would change if I just kept loving them. They didn't respond like I had hoped.

When they first started taking potshots at me, I wasn't sure how to react. Their attacks began as minor confrontations. I would humble myself and apologize, but my efforts to appease them were treated with indifference and contempt. Then I started hearing rumors of secret gatherings, where I was obviously the subject of their conversations.

Business meetings that once were times of thanksgiving and praise suddenly became arenas of conflict. They started opposing ministry suggestions, which they had previously supported. Soon they began making surprise visits to my home with petty lists of "concerns." One of them kept showing up unannounced where my wife worked to spy on her.

Their grumblings became more frequent, intense, and widespread. It was as if they were examining me under a microscope, hoping to find something to criticize. Their continual criticisms tied my stomach in knots. I spent many sleepless nights, wondering what I had done to deserve their cruel treatment. Many times I asked myself, *Why hadn't I been warned about this when I was in Bible school?*

All I wanted to do was reach people for Christ. While I was pastor, the church more than tripled in attendance in less than two years, and offerings rose dramatically. We built a brand new facility, won hundreds of people to Christ and were among the leaders in baptisms in the State of Michigan. Due to our rapid growth, I was selected as a church growth consultant with the Southern Baptist Convention Sunday School Board in Michigan.

Things were never better for all of us, so you would think everyone would be thrilled, right? Wrong. With so many new people joining, the old guard was losing control of "their" church and was furious at me for being responsible. In sheer desperation, I confided in a man who had previously been a friend and supporter. I didn't know that he was a spy sent by the abusers to obtain information. After some strategic collaborating, they were ready to drop the bomb.

It culminated unexpectedly during a Wednesday night business meeting. What hurt most was that my children, my wife, and my parents were all there to witness the demolition of someone they loved. I'll never forget the look of disbelief in the eyes of my family as contrived allegations were fired at me with machine gun rapidity.

I now know what a lynch mob looks like. As I helplessly searched for compassion in the faces of those I had often assisted, I received hate and anger in return. They accused me of lying, but never cited an example. They accused me of stealing, although it was impossible. I never touched an offering and couldn't even sign a check. The viciousness of their allegations impugned my integrity and undermined my effectiveness as a pastor.

I can't tell you how abandoned I felt as I sat silently with my face buried in my hands and let them attack me—the one whom God called to be their shepherd! They knew that if they could make my life miserable, they could drive me away. They were right. I couldn't put my family through any more of their excruciating torment, so I submitted my resignation.

I had my family to support, yet I had no opportunities for employment, nowhere to go, and no idea what I was going to do the rest of my life. But did any of that bother the ones who forced me out? No. They were glad I was gone.

Stopping the Insanity
The sign of a sick church is the revolving door of ministerial turnover, while the ones who kicked the pastors out remain in power. Consequently, any minister invited to serve in that congregation will probably be moving again in less than three years. An abused pastor shared this report with us:

> After that small faction started fighting me, I decided to research the history of the church to see how long this had been going on. I went back to 1945 and discovered that I was their twenty-second pastor since the end of WWII, for an average stay of just over 2.5 years each. When I shared this with the church council, the antagonists saw nothing abnormal with the frequent pastor turnover. That short tenure of the pastorate was normal in their eyes.

Many shepherds have tried to cooperate with the anti-pastor coalition, hoping to ease tensions and resolve differences. But no matter how many concessions pastors make to please these mobsters, it only serves to delay the inevitable. In pastor abusers' minds, termination of the minister is the only viable "solution" to the problem.

Ross Campbell, a psychiatrist who has worked with many terminated ministers says, "Termination can happen to any minister no matter how good he is. The more ministers are compassionate or are servant pastors, the more vulnerable they are. If you get a mean, sociopathic board member, it's easy to manipulate a pastor. This is happening to our best, most wonderful pastors."[14]

This vicious cycle of hiring and firing pastors must be stopped. But how? Although I will give numerous suggestions throughout this book, the bottom-line cure is found in God's Word:

> Obey your leaders, and submit to them; for they keep watch over your souls, as those who will give an account. Let them do this with joy and not with grief, for this would be unprofitable for you. (Heb. 13:17)

Because pastor abusers rarely repent, they will remain entrenched in power until someone unseats them. As shepherds continue to be battered, they ask themselves, *When will the silent majority of godly church members join together and excommunicate these bullies?*

Until that question is answered, Satan will gleefully keep notching his gun with the names of God's shepherds—who were destroyed by the very people they came to lead.

---

[14] O'Brien, Robert. "When Ministers Are Forced Out, Ministry Group Ready to Step In." Adapted from stories by Alberta Lindsey in the Richmond (VA) Times-Dispatch and David Winfrey in the Western Recorder.

Chapter 2

Satan's Strategy to Expel the Pastor

And indeed, all who desire to live godly in Christ Jesus will be persecuted. (2 Tim. 3:12)

By the time you finish reading this book more than a hundred fellow pastors will have been tossed to the curb with nowhere to go and no one to turn to. Glenn Booth, a church consultant, relates the following tragic story about an unjustly dismissed pastor:

> In his six years at the church, Sunday school and worship attendance doubled, enrollment tripled, offerings more than doubled and the church built two new buildings. Yet the pastor was fired because a few long-time church members liked things the way they used to be.
> Here's a man now facing difficulty; maybe never even being considered by another church because he's been terminated by this one. This is a man who has gone through seminary, discovered how to do things right, did them right, had the kind of success every minister would dream of, and yet ended up being fired.[15]

This isn't an isolated case. It's happening to God's servants with far more regularity than is ever made known to the public. We aren't ignorant of the devil's schemes. To halt a church where God's Word is preached and lives are being changed, Satan's sinister strategy is quite simple: keep assaulting the Lord's messenger and don't let up.

Every pastor needs to understand that persecution is part of the job description for preaching the gospel. The apostle Paul was stoned, beaten times without number, scourged on five occasions, and locked up in prison. He didn't receive such rough treatment as punishment for doing wrong, but as persecution for doing right. He was the bull's-eye on Satan's hit list.

Although you probably anticipated opposition from "out there" in the unbelieving world, you weren't expecting your persecution to come

---

[15] Glenn Booth, "Healing Broken Ministers" *Southwestern News*.

from *within* the church. The reality, however, is that your adversaries are not only in the church, but are often running it. The devil assails pastors through willing accomplices within the congregation who are trying their best to intimidate and discourage you. A pastor said:

> After I had been their pastor about six months, I gave an altar call and twelve people came forward to receive Christ. When I came into the office the next day, the matriarch of church was waiting for me. She told me, "If you ever do anything like that again, I will stop the altar call by myself if I have to. We will not have evangelistic services in this church on Sunday morning!"
>
> Not long after this, one of the main controllers tried to pick a fight with me. He came at me with his fists clenched and was trying to get me to fight him. I said, "You're not going to get me to fight you. You need to leave this office." But he wouldn't leave. He kept coming at me with his fists clenched like he was going to swing, trying to get me to swing first. I had to call 911 to get him to leave.

Because of your position as the congregation's spiritual leader, you're going to be a target of Satan, just like Paul. The devil will fight against everything you stand for because it's totally against his dark agenda.

Don't let that unnerve you because God is certainly aware of the hostility you face. After the apostles were flogged for preaching Jesus, they considered it a privilege to be persecuted, and went away "rejoicing that they had been considered worthy to suffer shame for His name" (Acts 5:41).

Keep this verse in mind as you read about Satan's strategy to mistreat God's messengers. Don't be ignorant of the devil's tactics, and always remember that the Lord will reward you for serving Him amidst opposition.

Modern-Day Persecution

Not all persecution involves being burned at the stake. America's pastors may not be scourged or stoned, but they're persecuted in other ways—through nonstop criticism, malicious slander, and unjustifiable termination. One counselor observed, "I spend a lot of my time with corporations in downsizing. I haven't seen any of them treating their employees like I'm seeing churches treating [pastors]."[16]

Tragically, it's much easier to be fired from a church than it is from a secular job. While we whole-heartily agree that immoral, corrupt pastors should be terminated, too many upright pastors are fired simply because a few church bullies don't like his personality or ministry philosophy. And what's even more astonishing—no matter how badly a church mistreated its former pastor, a multitude of ministerial candidates are quick to send in their resumes to replace him.

If you were suddenly dismissed from the pastorate, what would you do? How long would it take to find a church that's eager to hire someone who has been fired? If you search for a secular job, where can you transfer your skills? How many professions besides churches are looking for someone to preach, teach the Bible, translate Greek, and visit the sick? If you do find another vocation, you'll probably start at the bottom. How will you pay your bills and feed your family in the meantime? As you probably know, terminated clergy aren't eligible to receive unemployment. Where will you live and where will your children attend school?

Forced termination casts the displaced pastor in the most desperate and devastating financial crisis he will probably ever experience. It will be extremely difficult for him to find a comparable job because his termination makes him look like damaged goods.

"You never regain your money," an ex-pastor explained. "Financially, you're devastated."[17]

An abused pastor explained how the persecution cost him his inheritance:

> A small, hateful group in my church pressured me to resign. It was a year and a half before another church hired me, but my salary was substantially less. During my time of unemployment, we depleted our savings of many thousands of dollars, which I had inherited from my parents. I wanted to save the inheritance for my retirement, but I had to spend most of it on living expenses during those months I was searching for a new place to go.

---

[16] Winfrey, David. "Pastors falling prey to leader-hostile environment." *Western Recorder*. October 7, 1997.

[17] Marv Knox, "'I'll tell you it hurts,' pastor says of forced termination" *Baptist Standard*.

It may take months, or even years, to find another church that's willing to take a risk on hiring a pastor who was kicked out. An unjustly fired minister sent out resumes for four years before another church hired him:

> I was forced out of my church by some mean deacons, who also ran off my predecessor. Over the next four years, I sent my resume to 120 churches. It took four years for me to find another church that would call me to be their pastor. Apparently all those search committees thought I had done something wrong or immoral because I hadn't been a pastor for a long time.

Being forced to sell a home at an inopportune time is another financial nightmare that nearly all terminated clergy must face. A pastor shared how he borrowed a large sum of money to fix up his house, only to find himself putting it up the "For Sale" sign less than a year and a half later:

> After I became their pastor, we bought a house that needed a lot of repairs and spent thousands of dollars fixing it up. We were in it just 17 months when they fired me. We were forced to sell our house and lost over $30,000 on the deal. We pretty much lost everything. We walked away from that situation with nothing in the bank. We were broke. We moved in with a retired couple in the church for a few months because I didn't have a job. Because of their abuse, in just a matter of weeks I had lost nearly everything—my church, my job, my house, and my money.

Perhaps no other situation is as unique and hopeless as the ousted pastor. And this is why Satan creates an insurgency to drive clergy out of the ministry.

You might not have been told this in Bible school or seminary, dear pastor, but this fate lurks in the shadows for all who are on Satan's hit list. Ironically, the targets on Satan's hit list and the servants on God's honor roll are the same names!

God promises an incredible eternal reward for pastors who take care of His flock. First Peter 5:4 says, "When the Chief Shepherd appears, you will receive the unfading crown of glory."

Satan's Six-Step Strategy to Drive Out the Pastor

The devil's modus operandi isn't hard to figure out, as we've heard the same scenario repeated in congregations throughout the country. The enemy plants troublemakers in churches who join forces together to resist the pastor's leadership. The procedure to force the minister out and take control of a church requires six steps.

Step #1 Plant troublemakers in congregations.

All forced exits of innocent pastors have the same thing in common—antagonists within the church instigated their departure. Before that can ever happen, the abusers must first make their way into the fellowship. The apostle Paul exposed the first step, "Satan disguises himself as an angel of light. Therefore it is not surprising if his servants also disguise themselves as servants of righteousness" (2 Cor. 11:14-15).

Vance Havner once said, "Satan is not fighting churches; he is joining them. He does more harm by sowing tares than by pulling up wheat. He accomplishes more by imitation." The enemy cleverly plants his henchmen in congregations, who are often voted into seats of power. A Southern Baptist pastor explained the reason he was driven out of his church. "My congregation was armed with WMD's—World's Meanest Deacons."

For too long we've looked the other way in an attempt to deny what is painfully obvious; Satan has planted troublemakers inside churches for the purpose of wreaking havoc in God's kingdom. If the devil's goal is to take down the church, which person will be the primary target? Take a look in the mirror, pastor.

Kenneth Haugk calls these ungodly controllers "antagonists." In his book, *Antagonists in the Church*, Haugk states:

> Antagonists are individuals who, on the basis of non-substantive evidence, go out of their way to make insatiable demands, usually attacking the person or performance of others. These attacks are selfish in nature, tearing down rather than building up, and are frequently directed against those in a leadership capacity.[18]

---

[18] Haugk, Kenneth. *Antagonists in the Church*, Minneapolis, MN: Augsburg Publishing House, 1988, 21-22.

Antagonists operate with a protracted history of animosity and total disrespect for the office of pastor. One former minister told us, "After I had moved my family from Texas to be their pastor, an angry woman who helped force my termination kept referring to me as 'that plague from Texas who infected our church.'" How can anyone who disrespects the office of pastor ever unite a church or expand God's kingdom?

Step #2 Bring the troublemakers together to build an anti-pastor network.

After the troublemakers infiltrate the church, Satan rallies them together to build a guerrilla army that will resist the pastor's leadership. Although the abusers may stand independently at first, they'll eventually find each other, form a network, and recruit others to join their cause. Absalom, the son of David, followed step two when he built his anti-king army that would displace his father from the throne: "And the conspiracy was strong, for the people increased continually with Absalom" (2 Sam. 15:12).

Complainers instinctively gravitate toward other discontented members. They'll get together for coffee and will become giddy and invigorated to discover they're both miffed at the pastor over the same issues. Instantly, an unbreakable bond develops between them, and they phone each other for a daily dose of gossip. They're amazed at how much they think alike, which reinforces the idea in their minds that they're right.

They'll drop hints to others, testing the waters to see if they would like to be enlisted in their subversive army. As more disgruntled members are recruited, the coalition grows in strength. Once the anti-pastor army is large enough, a line is drawn in the sand, separating those for and against the pastor.

In many churches, this group of insubordinate people have been members the longest and they're convinced their right to rule is based on their tenure instead of Scripture. These rebellious members won't obey their pastors because they view ministerial staff simply as church employees that *they* pay. Consequently, they see themselves as the bosses, which justifies their disrespect for the God-established position. Such an unbiblical setting creates a gallery of onlookers, each with a yardstick in which to measure the pastor's performance.

These power brokers, who consider themselves the "owners" of the church, work through intimidation. They want the preacher to know they can get force him out at any time if he refuses to bow down to their orders. This tactic goes back two thousand years. The Pharisees threatened to kick people out of their synagogues if they got out of line: "Nevertheless many even of the rulers believed in Him, but because of the Pharisees they were not confessing Him, *lest they should be put out of the synagogue*; for they loved the approval of men rather than the approval of God" (John 12:42-43).

In small churches, the power brokers are usually the charter members or a particular family who feel they must control the church until their dying day. Since they were church members *before* the pastor arrived on the scene (being "grandfathered in"), they believe that authority is based on "who was here first" instead of scriptural mandates. They conjure up their power and counterfeit spiritual authority through witchcraft, by using an unholy spirit to manipulate, dominate, and control others.

Nobody knows the misery pastors endure at the hands of these insurgents except other pastors. Although they claim to the church's true leaders, they're no different than Korah, who opposed Moses and Aaron (see Num. 16:1-40).

Step #3 Promote the most confrontational members to lead the rebellious group.

Every army needs a general, so the devil chooses a ringleader within the church, usually a deacon, board member, or someone of influence, who can be the hardnosed spokesperson for the other unhappy members. Absalom proceeded with step three, and volunteered to be the spokesman for the discontented: "Oh, that one would appoint me judge in the land, then every man who has any suit or cause could come to me, and I would give him justice" (see 2 Sam. 15:2-4).

If the "chosen one" is a layperson who doesn't hold an office of authority, he will bring his protests to church board members, claiming to represent a large number of members who are upset with the pastor's performance. The spokesperson will manipulate the weakest board members, who are most likely to give in to the antagonists' demands.

Pastor abusers are frequently viewed by others as the "pillars" of the church, though they may not hold official roles. Jean Leeman, who manages the Bethel Pastoral Centre for recovery from congregational abuse says, "They are in power positions because of a long connection with the church, or their forebears gave money, or they did. So people stand back and let them take over."[19]

It's astounding how easily unqualified laymen can advance into leadership when integrity and a submissive heart are overlooked. It's not uncommon for wealthy members to be in positions of church authority. There's nothing wrong with that. But if their hearts aren't right, they'll convince themselves that they've earned the right to rule by the large sums they give.

A domineering businessman can be elected to a church board simply because of his standing in the community. If he doesn't have a heart of humility, he'll often be the one who bosses the pastor around. Sometimes rebellious people can gain control of a church simply by volunteering for an office that no one else wants.

Once this appointee gets positioned in the place of prominence, it's almost impossible to unseat him. To prevent ungodly people from gaining authority, Paul gave this warning: "Do not lay hands upon anyone too hastily and thus share responsibility for the sins of others; keep yourself free from sin" (1 Tim. 5:22).

After a church has put its stamp of approval on the highly-opinionated candidate, he arrogantly views himself as the church boss. And this is the root of the pastor abuser problem—unqualified, ungodly people holding positions of authority.

Step #4 Attack the pastor's character to make him look like the church's enemy.

We find this fourth step played out in the Book of Acts. Stephen was lied about and slandered by a malicious mob that was determined to stop him, even if it required murder:

> Then they secretly induced men to say, "We have heard him (Stephen) speak blasphemous words against Moses and against God." And they stirred up the people . . . and they put forward false witnesses who said, "This man incessantly speaks against this holy place, and the Law" (Acts 6:9, 11-13).

---

[19] "Bullied clergy seek respite" by Barney Zwartz, November 13, 2005. www.theage.com.au/news/national/bullied-clergy-seek-respite/2005/11/12/1131578275984.html

Slander is one of the devil's most effective tools, and we find the slander factor actively at work in churches today. One pastor enjoyed several years of effective ministry—growth in attendance, a successful building program, strong church stewardship, and happy relationships. Then he was fired after a few individuals smeared his reputation. He explained:

> That small group got against me. They started lying. They said I was a gambler. And then they attacked my wife. When they can't get anything on the minister, they go after his wife or his children. Only by suspending the bylaws were they able to fire me.[20]

For the unsuspecting and unlearned, perception is reality. Facts aside, over extended periods when incessant, besmirching innuendo is leveled against a targeted individual, it rearranges the thinking of those who are privy to it. One clear and undisputed master at this was Adolph Hitler's Minister of Public Enlightenment and Propaganda, Joseph Goebbels.

Goebbels was well educated, and held a doctor of philosophy degree from Heidelberg University. Seeking to brainwash an entire population, he implemented the "Big Lie" technique of mass propaganda, which is still operating today: "People will believe a big lie sooner than a little one; and if you repeat it frequently enough, people will sooner or later believe it."

Employing coolly calculated speeches laden with biting anti-Semitic humor and epithets, he systematically devalued Jews and programmed the populace to detest them. When the time came for their imprisonment and extermination, the brainwashed Germans nodded with approval as six million people were led to the incinerators.

The same diabolical technique convinced the multitude to crucify the Lord Jesus. In spite of the fact He performed righteous works and lived a sinless life, the people demanded that He be put to death. Their perception of Him as an enemy of tradition and organized religion far outweighed His innocence, making crucifixion the only sensible solution.

With that in mind, it's not surprising when pastors are slandered by members of their own congregations. Often the reputations of innocent clergy are tarnished beyond repair. All it takes to destroy a

---

[20] Knox.

pastor is to put a question mark in people's minds that the false allegations *might* be true.

Step #5 Execute the battle plan.
The crusade to overthrow the pastor requires a methodical, well-executed plan. David revealed step five in Psalm 64:5-6, "They hold fast to themselves an evil purpose; they talk of laying snares secretly. They say, 'Who can see them?' They devise injustices, saying, 'We are ready with a well-conceived plot.'"

Barney Self, a former pastoral counselor with LifeWay Christian Resources, handled 4,300 distress calls from pastors in eight years. Because the stories sounded so much alike, he claimed he could "finish the details" after hearing a just brief summary of the account.[21]

In my interviews with pastors, I was shocked to discover similar pastor abuse scenarios taking place in churches across the country, even though they occurred in different denominations that had no way of communicating with each other. I can only conclude that the warfare against pastors isn't instigated by flesh and blood, but from the realm of spiritual darkness. Satan has orchestrated a script for pastor abusers to follow, which is transmitted to them by planting evil thoughts in their hearts.

Satan's Advice to Pastor Abusers

The devil's instruction to the abusers goes as follows:

- **Be an astute church politician.** Get as many people as possible on your side, who will be your allies when the confrontation begins.
- **Keep a running list of problems.** Call them "concerns" but never be too specific.
- **Introduce trial balloon statements.** Example: "I'm not sure I agree with pastor's decision to (fill in the blank)." Listen carefully to the person's response. If the individual agrees, add that name to your ally list and provide him or her with more ammunition.
- **Show public disrespect.** Roll your eyes whenever the pastor says something you don't agree with. This lets others know you think

---

[21] *The Christian Index*, January 31, 2008, 6.

he's stupid, which builds loyalty with other rebels like a secret handshake.

- **Sympathize with complainers.** Eagerly listen to all complaints without challenging their validity. Volunteer to be their spokesperson, just as Absalom sat at the gate and became the voice for the discontented.
- **Organize secret meetings.** Select a private location for an evening get-together. Invite only those who have expressed anger and discontentment. Overstate church problems and blame the pastor. Be sure to tell them, "I'm not getting my needs met."
- **Recruit a spy.** Find an undercover agent who will befriend the pastor and pretend to be on his side. The spy's job is to acquire any information that can be distorted and used against him. Bring the report back to the chief abuser. This is an effective tactic, but only if the spy can hide his real motives. My servants, the Pharisees, sent spies to trick Jesus, and my servant Tobiah hired Shemaiah to set up a trap to kill Nehemiah.[22] Unfortunately, the spies' intentions were discovered and the plots were foiled. However, it's much easier to get away with this in churches because they won't hold my abusers accountable.
- **Increase your assaults.** Persuade your allies to write demoralizing emails and letters to the pastor. It's best to leave them unsigned so his adversaries remain invisible and it keeps him wondering.
- **Distort the facts.** Mix in a little bit of truth so they can't figure out that you're lying. Keep repeating the same lies again and again, and the congregation will eventually suspect that it must be true.
- **Fudge the numbers.** Make your group of dissenters appear larger than his group of supporters by saying, "There are a lot more people like us who feel the same way." Of course, don't mention their names because we know it's only a few people.
- **Feign sorrow and grief.** Squash any sympathy for the pastor by telling them "more important issues" have to be dealt with. Make people believe that it hurts you to get rid of the pastor, but someone has to do it "for the good of the church."
- **Manipulate the vote.** Make visits and phone calls. Use threats, if necessary, to get the needed votes. Contact the inactive members who never attend church but still have the right to vote. Convince

---

[22] Luke 20:20, Neh. 6:9-13.

them that the pastor is about to destroy the church and it's their Christian duty to vote him out.

- **Put the pastor on trial.** Be furious and intimidating in the final confrontation. The best way to cross-examine him is to falsify and exaggerate information about him so that he's forced to clarify and justify himself. This makes him look guilty and defensive.
- **Push for termination.** Deflect the pastor's attempts to reconcile. Keep the focus on his inadequacies to create the illusion that the only solution is to get rid of the pastor. Do not accept reconciliation because your goal is *termination*.

Although the above agenda sounds outrageous, you'd be surprised how many clergy will bear witness to the fact that a similar scenario has occurred in their congregations. A Baptist pastor explained how he was fired by a small group of deacons who manipulated the vote:

> Our church grew over fifty percent after I became pastor, but some of the longtime members didn't like the new people joining. They got together and devised a plan to stop the growth. When 115 people visited our church in one year, I wondered why hardly any of the visitors ever came back for a second visit. I had noticed that every week our older members, who had given me so much trouble, were inviting the first-time visitors out to lunch after church. As I followed up on our visitors, they told me that the older members had taken them to lunch and spent the entire time complaining about me! The visitors had to be thinking, *If his own members don't like him, why should I visit that church again?*
>
> Even in that turbulent environment, I still had a vision for the church and wanted to do my best to cooperate with the deacons who opposed me. My wife and I, along with some of my supporters, scheduled a meeting with the deacons to talk about issues and try to make peace with them. We thought our prayers had been answered when the chairman of the deacons called for the other deacons, who had been fighting me, to support my ministry and vision for the church. However, it was just one month later when the deacon chairman pushed for me to resign.
>
> The faction that hated me called all the inactive members and asked them to show up for the business meeting to vote me out as pastor. People came to that meeting who hadn't attended the church one time in over two years that I was there. In many Baptist churches, members can be on the rolls, and even though they never attend church or participate in activities—they can still vote! An

overwhelming number of people showed up for this meeting whom I hadn't seen before. These inactive members only show up at church to be the swing votes, doing as they've been instructed by the unhappy members.

My 16-year old and 7-year old daughters were in that meeting, and watched in horror as the hot-headed members verbally attacked me. I resigned as pastor that night. Even though it has been over a year since I left the church, my daughter is still deeply disturbed by what happened in that meeting. As we have gone through the healing process, she has shared with me that she's still angry that those church people could talk to her daddy in that way.

A pastor in Texas shared with us a similar story how he was forced out of his church by the votes of inactive members.

Over the past few years, I received a number of hateful emails from individuals who opposed me. They spread lies and slandered me all over town. On the day of the vote, all the inactive members showed up to vote against me. Many people who came to vote had not been in church in years, some as much as twenty, I was told. Over double our normal attendance showed up to vote which was enough to change the outcome. Afterward, one man squeezed my hand, crushing the ends of my fingers together. Through gritted teeth he growled, "Are you going to leave now?"

An Ohio pastor told us that his church was in the process of changing their bylaws so that only active members would be able to vote. When the abusers caught wind of this, they quickly launched the plan to fire him.

I had been reaching out to people of other races and thirty African-American children came to know Christ. Some of the members didn't like it and decided to get rid of me.

At a Wednesday night business meeting, the power bloc showed up with a bunch of inactive members they had rounded up. Most of them I had never seen before. I had seen a few of them at a potluck dinner, but never at a worship service. Because they were still on the church rolls, they could vote. A deacon in that group made a motion from the floor to remove me as pastor. I was fired that night because I lost by two votes.

I was promised a month's salary in severance pay, even though the faction didn't want to give me anything. I would not have even received that, if it weren't for one of the men on the stewardship committee who supported me.

Step #6 After the pastor is removed, keep the abusers entrenched in power.

Once the pastor is terminated, the abusers will have established themselves in power and will fight every shepherd that God sends their way. The rejection of the Lord's messengers, which began with "prophet abuse" in the Old Testament, continues as "pastor abuse" in the New Testament Church.

We see the sixth step clearly depicted in 2 Chron. 36:15-16, "And the Lord, the God of their fathers, sent word to them again and again by His messengers . . . but *they continually mocked the messengers of God*, despised His words and *scoffed at His prophets*."

The unending cycle of prophet abuse is also portrayed in Christ's parable of the landowner who planted a vineyard and went on a journey.

> "And at the harvest time he sent a slave to the vine-growers . . . but the vine-growers *beat him and sent him away* empty-handed. And he proceeded to send another slave; and *they beat him also* and treated him shamefully, and sent him away empty-handed. And he proceeded to send a third; and *this one also they wounded and cast out*" (Luke 20:10-12).

The slaves represent God's prophets, while the vine-growers symbolize the stubborn religious leaders who opposed them. It didn't matter how many messengers the Lord sent their way, the prophet abusers rejected them all—assaulting them and sending them away empty-handed.

Is this not a picture of an abusive church? After the pastor abusers have beaten up and kicked out one pastor, they'll continue to mistreat every shepherd the Lord sends to that church—and throw them out empty-handed, without a severance agreement. A terminated pastor said:

> The pastor who preceded me had difficulty leading and working with certain members because of a powerful group that opposed him. I soon discovered that gossip, rumors, and lies were spread about me by the same members who had caused the previous pastor's resignation.

With the election of a new deacon chairman who was openly antagonistic to me, I also was forced to resign.

Another pastor was the fourth in a line of abused shepherds.

When I accepted the call to the church, I didn't know that the three pastors before me had been forced out. My predecessor had his car spray-painted. In spite of this, the denomination never warned me about the church's abusive history. Their philosophy was, "We don't want to tell you about how the church mistreated its pastors because it will color your perspective. Maybe you'll have a different experience than your predecessors." Well, now we know better. They forced me out two years later.

Because few churches exercise church discipline, pastor abusers are rarely held accountable for their actions. This emboldens them to keep attacking God's shepherds, knowing that no one will challenge their despicable behavior. Eventually someone must take a stand against the abusers and hold them accountable, or their attacks will never end. Church discipline is essential if we're ever going to solve the pastor abuser problem.

Strike the Shepherd

Pastor, what may have been unclear before is not a secret any longer. Satan wants to drive you away so he can stop God's work and cripple the church. Jesus told His disciples, "You will all fall away, because it is written, 'I will strike down the shepherd, and the sheep shall be scattered'" (Mark 14:27). Notice that true sheep follow the shepherd and when the leader is taken out, the followers are thrown into disarray.

Satan knows you can potentially influence many people to follow Christ. If he can force you out of the church, those who are being encouraged by your ministry will become disillusioned. Like a bowling ball hitting the first pin, all the other pins will tumble as well.

The more that God uses you to further His kingdom, the bigger target you become on Satan's hit list. But remember, at the same time you're being attacked, the Lord is promoting you on His honor roll for greater eternal reward. He is fully aware of the turmoil that you are experiencing and will show you how to proceed through it.

Chapter 3

The Driving Forces Behind Pastor Abuse

"But beware of men; for they will deliver you up to the courts, and scourge you in their synagogues."(Matt. 10:17)

My local Christian radio station asked its listeners to send them a short note of encouragement about their pastor, which would be read on the air during Clergy Appreciation Month. After weeks of pleas to the audience with little response, the frustrated general manager told me, "I just don't understand it. We have eight hundred churches in our listening area, and not one person from over ninety percent of the congregations sent us a note."

"That should tell you something," I replied. "Many church members think pastors don't need to be appreciated because we're getting paid. They have no idea how stressful it is to pastor a church and put up with difficult people. Some church members are trying to pressure their pastor to leave, and if they showed appreciation, it might encourage him to stay longer."

Few people understand what it's like to be constantly bombarded with criticisms and rarely encouraged or thanked. Dave Goetz, former editor of *Leadership Journal*, states that "It needs to be said that churches simply don't know how to love pastors. They really don't trust them to make long-term decisions for the betterment of the church. They want leaders, but as soon as they get them, they have a compulsion to bring them down."[23]

Lest we be misunderstood, we need to say again what pastor abuse is not. It's not being abusive to terminate a pastor for sexual immorality, stealing offerings, drunkenness, teaching heresy, shirking responsibilities, being rebellious and defiant, or acting like a cruel dictator—which are legitimate grounds to expel someone on church

---

[23] Winfrey, David. "Pastors falling prey to leader-hostile environment.'" Western Recorder. October 7, 1997.

staff. When a minister engages in unethical practices, he disqualifies himself from serving as pastor.

Those issues aside, pastor abuse occurs when the minister has done little or nothing wrong, yet is undeservedly slandered, mistreated, and criticized by a rebellious faction within the congregation. It's the persecution of God's servant by unappeasable sociopaths, who force a pastor from a church every six minutes.[24]

Pastor abuse isn't something suddenly sprung upon this generation. The persecution of God's spokesmen has been going on for thousands of years in a variety of cultural settings. While the enemy tries to discourage the Lord's messengers by viciously mistreating them, God counteracts the devilish strategy by graciously rewarding His faithful servants for enduring hardship.

Jesus instructed His disciples to leap for joy when they were hated, slandered, and ostracized. "Blessed are you when men hate you, and ostracize you, and cast insults at you, and spurn your name as evil, for the sake of the Son of Man. Be glad in that day, and leap for joy, for behold, your reward is great in heaven; for *in the same way their fathers used to treat the prophets*" (Luke 6:22-23).

The mistreatment of God's servants has been perpetuated ever since the days of the Old Testament prophets. Back then, it would be called prophet abuse instead of pastor abuse. Remarkably, the tactics applied centuries ago against prophets are uncannily similar to those used on pastors today. Christ said "in the same way" (their methods haven't changed) "their fathers" (previous generations) "used to treat the prophets" (God's messengers).

You're probably wondering why someone in the family of God claiming to love the Lord would want to abuse anyone, much less the pastor. Like all obsessive personalities, pastor abusers have their rationale for what they do, and are intensely driven by a self-serving agenda and an unwavering compulsion to bring down the shepherd.

Jesus warned us to be wary of men's motives: "But beware of men; for they will deliver you up to the courts, and scourge you in their synagogues."(Matt. 10:17). Now get this—it's the religious people, not the atheists, who will whip His followers in the very place they claim to worship God, and feel justified in doing it!

---

[24] Rediger, Lloyd. *Clergy Killers.* Louisville, KY: Westminster John Knox Press, 1997, 6.

Those who inflict persecution on ministers truly believe they're serving God. Jesus said, "They will make you outcasts from the synagogue, but an hour is coming for everyone who kills you to *think that he is offering service to God.*" (John 16:2). Tragically, their perverted orders come from hell, not heaven. Some that have gained positions of authority in the Lord's house shouldn't even be there. The apostle Paul unjustly suffered because of the threats of "false brethren" (2 Cor. 11:26).

God's shepherds today aren't ministering in synagogues but in churches. Like the religious people who scourged the disciples inside their synagogues, there's no shortage of counterfeit saints who are more than willing to mistreat pastors inside their houses of worship. Paying no attention to Biblical warnings or their own conscience, they administer punishment on their innocent targets.

Because the wheat and tares will grow up together until Jesus returns, pastors will always be plagued by the tyrannical few. The pastor haters want you gone for one or more of the following reasons. Please note that not every reason listed below will apply to your church, but we must cover all the causes because every situation is different.

1. Unrealistic Expectations

Church members who have unrealistic expectations for their minister will unleash harsh criticism and slanderous gossip if he fails to meet their every demand. "Unrealistic expectations" creates an *impossible job description* for the pastor, which no human on the planet can fulfill. This ridiculous job description forms the eyeglasses through which clergy abusers view their shepherd's every action.

People often have a picture in their minds of the perfect pastor. After a while, they realize he isn't the perfect pastor, but an imperfect person. When this realization occurs, they will either tear up the picture, or they will tear up the pastor.

Perhaps you've heard the job description of the ideal minister:

> The ideal pastor preaches exactly twenty minutes with an hour's content. He condemns sin, but never offends anyone. He works from 8 a.m. to midnight, and also serves as the church janitor. He makes $40 a week, wears good clothes, and donates $30 a week to the church. He is 29 years old and has 40 years of experience. He is a strong leader, yet also follows everyone's advice. He can effectively relate to all teenagers, and spends all of his time with the elderly. He is tall and

short, thin and heavyset, and has one brown eye and one blue eye. He makes 15 house calls a day, regularly visits the hospital, and is always in his office.

The first time I read that I laughed. Every time since then I've winced a bit. The qualifications are ridiculous, and yet you would be surprised at just how many people have this job description in their minds when they call their pastor.

Unrealistic expectations always produce unreasonable criticisms. Pastor abusers will dissect the shepherd using the surgical knife of fault-finding. They will claim his sermons are too long ("he's longwinded") or not long enough ("he needs to put in more time preparing his messages"). They will complain about his leadership ("he's a dictator and doesn't listen to anyone") or his lack of leadership ("he has no vision and doesn't lead"). The abusers claim they want him to be a leader, yet they'll demand that he must follow their advice before making any decision, no matter how minor it may be. This puts him in a "no win" situation where he'll never please his critics.

They'll point out what he's not doing right. He's evangelistic, but doesn't feed the flock. He teaches the flock, but doesn't evangelize the lost. He spends too much time in his office instead of visiting people. He spends too much time visiting people and is never in his office. He's a great preacher, but a horrible administrator. He's a great administrator, but a horrible preacher.

One pastor said this about a critical member in his new church:

> He offered to take me out to eat one day, so I accepted. Little was I prepared for what was about to happen. Setting down his sandwich he said, "Brian, there are a number of things you are doing wrong, but for the sake of time I've kept my list to ten."[25]

With the spirit of discontentment ruling their hearts, no pastor will ever live up to such a grueling yardstick of unrealistic measurement. Like the guy at the carnival running back and forth spinning plates on sticks, the minister will wear himself out trying to please these fault-finding members. They expect him to have supernatural knowledge whenever a church member is sick, going through a difficulty, or just wants him to make a visit to their home. Then they are highly offended

---

[25] Jones, Brian. "When you feel like quitting vocational ministry . . ." MinistryToolBox, Issue #268, www.pastors.com, July 19, 2006.

when he doesn't come, even though no one has contacted him about their need.

One day when I was a young boy in the late 1950's, I was running a high fever. My mother called our doctor, who later showed up at our house. He pulled his stethoscope out of his large, black physician's bag, and carefully listened to my heartbeat. It was still thumping! He instructed my mom to give me aspirin and plenty of fluids, and then left for his next house call.

Those were the good old days when everyone expected doctors to visit patients in their homes. Although the physician's house call provided a personal touch, it was an extremely time-consuming and inefficient way to care for patients.

Somewhere along the way, doctors' house calls ceased to exist. I'm not exactly sure how they became extinct, but maybe all the doctors in the country got together at some convention, took a vote, and unanimously agreed to put a halt to it. Perhaps it dawned on them that they had it all backwards—that the patients should be visiting the doctors rather than vice-versa.

Regardless, no one expects physicians to come to their homes today. The doctors no longer wait on the patients; the patients wait in a room for the doctors. A shift in thinking has taken place; the "house call" mentality of the past has been replaced by the present-day "waiting room" mentality.

Those with unrealistic expectations view the pastor's role akin to the "doctor-visit-the-house" job description of the 1950's. He is seen as their personal employee, where he must pay special attention to every church member and be their best friend. They want him to lead, but he must first get the approval of every member so that he doesn't offend anyone. In their minds, that's what he's paid to do.

This concept of the pastor's job description has been propagated for decades and even centuries, primarily because the membership of churches historically averaged less than a hundred. When a church has less than a hundred members, the full-time pastor can have a personal relationship with the sheep in his flock. However, it's impossible for a pastor of a congregation of three hundred or more members to give his personal attention to each person. He doesn't have enough time in the day to give quality time to every member of the church. If the pastor tries to fulfill this unrealistic role, it will prevent him from accomplishing what God has actually called him to do.

For the last few decades, a huge paradigm shift has taken place and many churches have experienced tremendous numerical growth. Because these churches have grown to the hundreds, thousands, and even ten thousands, the pastor's role has changed dramatically. Not only does he not have time to give individual attention to everyone, he must train the church members to take on new responsibilities.

No longer can he make all the house calls to every member's home, hospitals, and rest homes—as if the church membership were only eighty. His new role calls for him to multiply his effectiveness by training his members to fulfill *their* callings in ministry, which brings us back to the pastor abuse problem.

Those who view the pastor's job as a one-man show don't understand the biblical concept of "equipping the saints to do the work of ministry" and will fiercely attack the pastor if he shifts from the "minister does everything" role. A pastor told us:

> I had been trying to teach the church that everyone is a minister and that I would equip them to do the work of ministry. I was trying to teach them what it meant to really be the church, the Body of Christ. But they didn't like what I said. In one meeting, one man literally came over the table one night, got within eight inches of my face, and started yelling at me. "If you don't want to do the work we hire you to do, then get the hell out of here! We hire you to do the ministry, so you do it. You keep your mouth shut and you do what we tell you to do!"

Pastor abusers are uncomfortable with the concept of the congregation doing the work of ministry, and the shepherd as the one training them to do it. That's not the job description they have in their minds.

They also don't want the congregation to grow, largely because it ruins their concept of what a church should be—a tiny, close-knit group. When new members start joining, it's obvious that the shepherd must give some of his attention to the new sheep in the flock, which means he doesn't have as much time to spend with the existing members. This causes them to resent the new members who are joining the church and taking a piece of their pie. Another minister writes:

> As the congregation grew, one of (the older members) told me, "These new people don't love this church like we do." And when I

inevitably spent less time with the charter members to concentrate on growth, they became sharply critical of me, too."[26]

The abuse begins when the pastor becomes too busy to hold each hand and give every member his undivided attention. This shift in roles—from pastor-does-everything, to equipping the saints for ministry—leads to the denigration and vilification of the pastor: "He doesn't care about us. All he cares about is numbers. He just wants to be proud of having a bigger church." Of course, this isn't the truth at all, but simply a slanderous attack on their shepherd.

Those who gave the pastor the right hand of fellowship to invite him will often be the same ones to give the right fist of rejection to evict him. No sooner has he unpacked his boxes, he'll have to start packing them again. The hinge on the revolving church door screams for more oil, as it turns pastors out almost as quickly as it lets them in.

2. Struggle for Power

Pastor abusers are driven by the urge to be in control and will do anything necessary to keep from relinquishing their power. "They're power brokers trying to throw tantrums and get their way," says Lloyd Rediger.[27]

If you're reaching people with the gospel, the "control freaks" usually won't accept the new members because they view them as threats to their power base. When a congregation experiences numerical increase, it shrinks the abusers' sphere of influence as they become outnumbered. The dread of losing control incites them to bring down the person causing the increase. As hard as it is for an evangelical Christian to believe, this is one of the main reasons pastors are forced out when their church starts growing.

Barney Self, a former pastoral counselor, agrees that some churches will terminate pastors for causing growth. "I've known pastors to be fired for instituting an evangelism program because it's going to bring people into the church and they won't look like existing members," Self said.[28]

---

[26] Shelley, Marshall. *Well-Intentioned Dragons.* Minneapolis, MN: Bethany House, 1985, 43.
[27] Rediger, 13.
[28] *The Christian Index*, January 31, 2008, 6.

A pastor explained how the controllers were afraid of losing their power:

> When I became their pastor, I didn't realize that a small group of very mean people were in control of the church. When the Lord started blessing our church with numerical growth, this group became hostile toward me. They felt they were losing their power because the church was getting bigger and bigger. Instead of them being big fish in a little pond, they were becoming little fish in a big pond. They tried to stop the growth by treating our visitors in an unfriendly way. They wanted to keep the church small so they could keep their power. And the more the church grew, the more aggressive they became toward me.

Power-hungry congregants feel threatened when someone steps on their turf. When I lived in Florida I heard Floridians say, "I wish people from other states would quit moving here." Ironically, the Florida residents who lived there fifteen years ago said the same thing about *them* before they came. Their philosophy of life is "I'm happy here and I don't want anyone else crowding my space." These territorial residents think they own Florida, protecting their turf from all outsiders.

I once hung a hummingbird feeder on my back porch. My wife and I love to watch all those miniature creatures whirling around our house and refueling at our station. However, one particularly antagonistic hummingbird kept chasing off all the other birds that came near. That arrogant little bird was "territorial" and obviously thought that it owned the feeder. It ignored the fact that I supplied the red juice for all hummingbirds to enjoy.

Pastor abusers can also be territorial, thinking they own the church. They're like that unfriendly hummingbird and will chase off any visitor who trespasses on their property. They view new members as cockroaches raiding their personal pantry. When strangers join the fellowship, they have no interest in befriending them, but treat them as illegal aliens who need to be deported. These abusers forget that the Lord Jesus owns the church and invites all to come.

An ex-pastor explained how the established members in his church rejected the newcomers:

> When I first came to the church, it was running about 200 in attendance. It grew to 500. It had been a small, rural church, and we had rapid growth with a lot of new folks joining. Some older members

didn't like the new people coming in and changing their church. Many of the new members were younger and the older members didn't like them. They referred to them as "the outsiders."

We aren't fooled by the tricks of the devil, which are usually unmasked in Scripture. Jesus performed many miracles while the Pharisees watched. In spite of the insurmountable proof that God's hand was at work, they conspired together to kill Him. They were afraid that they would lose their place of power if too many people became believers. The following passage exposes their demonic strategy:

> Therefore the chief priests and the Pharisees convened a council, and were saying, "What are we doing? For this man is performing many signs. *"If we let Him go on like this, all men will believe in Him*, and the Romans will come and *take away both our place* and our nation." (John 11:47-48)

Two factors compelled the Pharisees to plot against Jesus: the growing number of believers and the fear of losing their place. These same spiritual dynamics are at work in many churches today, which is why pastors are persecuted by those who are obsessed with being in control.

God will hold those in charge to a stricter judgment, simply because their decisions affect so many people (see James 3:1). The Lord's shepherds are keenly aware that they'll answer to Him for the way they've used their authority. Every true shepherd seeks to follow the Lord's directions and is ever conscious of the fact he will be held accountable on Judgment Day for his obedience.

In contrast, pastor abusers are only concerned with being in power, and give no thought whatsoever to the terrifying judgment they will one day face for their actions. Because they don't fear God's wrath, nothing constrains them from attacking the Lord's messenger.

William Easum in his book, *Sacred Cows Make Gourmet Burgers*, writes:

> The life and spirit of established churches is being drained by mean-spirited people called *Controllers.* Controllers are those leaders who withhold permission or make it difficult for new ministries to start. . . Controllers not only do not want change; they also want to control

everything that happens. Usually they are against anything that they do not think of first or that does not serve their personal needs.[29]

When a pastor is called to a church, he assumes that he's been granted the leadership role. That's the definition of a shepherd—one who leads the flock. However, the power-hungry group also wants control of the church, which means they will sooner or later resist the pastor's leadership.

They'll drop hints and suggestions about matters that really shouldn't concern them. Although these control freaks may or may not hold official positions in the church, they must know everything before it happens and demand a vote on every new issue. Their mission is not to reach the lost, make disciples, or support their pastor. They have only one obsession—*to be in control of the church*. Ultimately the controllers pressure the pastor to submit to their demands or they'll force his exit.

How can this conflict be settled? Resolving any dispute requires two things: a respect for the hierarchical flowchart and a willingness to cooperate—both of which are found lacking in control freaks. That means the struggle for the reins of leadership will continue until Satan's assaulters are expelled from the congregation or the pastor is driven out of the church.

3. Fear of Change

If your congregation is in the midst of changing a doctrinal mindset, transitioning to a different worship style, or some other kind of change, you can expect conflict to come with it. Change, whether right or wrong, will always bring those who oppose it, and the pastor will be the one feeling the heat. After a pastor is called to a church, it's not unusual for him to be criticized simply because he does things differently than the previous pastor.

Although people can be intimidated by many different kinds of fear, one in particular torments many church controllers—the fear of change. New people, new ministries, new methods, new ideas, new pastor . . . anything with the word "new" in front of it becomes the greatest threat to those who don't like change. We are reminded of

---

[29] Easum, William M. *Sacred Cows Make Gourmet Burgers*. Nashville: Abingdon Press, 1995, 31,32,35.

Jesus' words: "No one puts *new* wine into *old* wineskins; otherwise the new wine will burst the skins . . . ." (Luke 5:37).

His ideas didn't set well with the rigid mindset of the Pharisees, who were fully entrenched in their religious system. The same dynamic still exists today. When God wants to bring a fresh approach and new life to a church, it will be resisted by those who prefer the status quo. So when the new pastor is called to their church and he does things slightly different from the routine, the old guard defends their wineskin with the tenacity of a bulldog.

Many of them worship the memory of days gone by. Their primary goal is to protect the church, exactly as they've always remembered it. They will violently resist any prospective ministry that breaks their mold and doesn't follow the established program and protocol. As a result, when the visionary pastor shares an innovative strategy for reaching people, he finds himself under attack by the old guard. Beneath the surface, two conflicting philosophies are waging war: *past memories* versus *future ministries*.

Worshipping the past can be a trap for any generation that looks backward instead of forward. God told Moses to make a bronze serpent in the wilderness to save the people from their poisonous snake bites. Whoever looked at the serpent would be saved, which became a picture of Jesus dying on the cross for our sins (see John 3:14). Centuries later, King Hezekiah destroyed Moses' bronze serpent (which they called "Nehushtan") because people started worshipping the relic instead of God (see Num. 21:5-9, 2 Kings 18:4).

Many churches today are filled with modern-day Nehushtans; methods and memorabilia from the past that serve no practical purpose other than being idols. It might be the order of service, a ritual, a dead program that's being sustained on life-support, a chant that's repeated, or a particular hymn that's been sung for decades at the invitation. It could be an object such as a stained glass window donated in memory of a cherished member, or an antiquated sanctuary building—which have become sacred cows that cannot be touched. Whatever the idol is, all hell breaks loose if it's moved or removed.

One pastor shared with us how he was nearly crucified by his abusers when he tried to replace the large, wooden pulpit with a smaller one to make more room for the altar call and prayer. The huge, beautiful pulpit had been an icon for decades, and the historians went berserk at the mere suggestion of downsizing it.

Which do you think the Lord regards as more important; pulpit or people? Tradition or ministry? Jesus gave the answer. "And thus you invalidated the word of God *for the sake of your tradition.* You hypocrites, rightly did Isaiah prophesy of you, saying, 'This people honors Me with their lips, but their heart is far away from Me. But in vain do they worship Me, teaching as doctrines the precepts of men.'" (Matt. 15:6-7).

This guarding of the past is actually idolatry, turning the church into an historical museum and the controllers as its curators. Because these longtime historians are dedicated to preserving the past, they view change as a greater enemy than Satan!

Not surprisingly, any adjustment to the established routine makes these curators furious. Shakespeare once said, "In time we hate that which we often fear." When pastors challenge their congregants to try new methods to reach the lost, those stuck in the rut of traditionalism come unglued. Rather than being fishers of men, they view themselves as the keepers of aquarium, thinking their job is to guard the fish tank.

Seeing change as something evil, they view the pastor as the catalyst who is ruining their congregation. It doesn't matter to them that the church must adapt its strategy to reach current and future generations with the gospel or the congregation will wither up and eventually die. They are only interested in themselves, and are determined to keep the church routine exactly as it has always been.

Many of these curators don't know how to communicate with anyone outside of their small circle of church friends. They have no idea how to talk to unbelievers in today's world, much less how to incorporate new believers into the fellowship. Should these people be running the church?

Yet, if you dare to touch their sacred cows, you'll find yourself on the butcher block. In their minds, the only way to prevent the enemy of change from destroying the idol of routine is to kill the messenger. Instead of standing on the promises, you'll be evicted from the premises.

One former pastor, who had been above reproach and successfully grew his church, was fired because he tried to rearrange the museum. He told us:

> I had made some needed changes over the years, all for good reasons. Our church had purchased a $40,000-$50,000 state-of-the-art audio and video system, but the traditionalists wouldn't allow me to use it

except to show words on the screen. They wouldn't let me show video clips for sermon illustrations because they called it "entertainment." They said, "You can't show movies because it's idolatry." I told them, "Why do we even have it then? We have all this technology but you won't let me use it."

Many of the older members, who had been there a long time, didn't want anything to change. We're talking about traditions that have nothing to do with Scripture. They defended it by saying, "But it's a tradition!" They crucified Jesus for violating their traditions, so I guess I'm in good company.

They kept going to their friends on the board with their complaints. Finally an elder came to me and said, "You're the best minister we've ever had. You study and every message is well-prepared. Your marriage and children are great, but you need to go because you've made too many changes, particularly in worship."

I had never been fired from a job my entire life and I didn't know what to do. They gave me a three-month severance package as long as I would keep quiet. If they perceived I was causing problems, they would cut it off. I've never gone back to being a pastor.

4. Opposing Visions

Another driving force behind pastor abuse is when a new vision is implemented—taking the church in an unfamiliar direction. When a pastor starts sharing the vision the Lord has lain upon his heart, the abusers are typically the first to resist it. Perhaps you've heard the following joke, which sadly reflects the resistance found in many churches.

A certain pastor believed God was calling the church to a new vision. At the next deacons' meeting, he presented his plan with as much conviction and passion as he could muster. When he finished, the deacon chairman called for a vote. All twelve deacons voted against the new vision, with only the pastor voting for it.

"Well, pastor, it looks like you'll have to rethink your vision," the deacon chairman said. "Would you like to close the meeting in prayer?"

The pastor raised his hands to heaven and prayed, "Lord, please show these people that it's not my vision but it's *your* vision!"

At that moment, the clouds darkened and a bolt of lightning shot through the window, splitting the table in two. The deacons were all knocked out of their chairs as the pastor remained standing unscathed.

As the deacons dusted themselves off, the chairman said, "Well, that's twelve votes to two now."

Many pastors face fierce opposition when they share the vision God has given them. Vision is the ability to see the direction the church is heading—what it will look like in the future. It's also a mindset, a way of thinking. For a church to accomplish God's will, the leaders and followers must "think the same" about how to reach people and glorify the Lord. Paul wrote to the Philippians:

> Only conduct yourselves in a manner worthy of the gospel of Christ; so that whether I come and see you or remain absent, I may hear of you that you are standing firm in one spirit, *with one mind striving together* for the faith of the gospel . . . make my joy complete by being *of the same mind*, maintaining the *same love, united in spirit, intent on one purpose.* (Phil. 1:27, 2:2)

When a husband and wife think alike about issues, conflicts and disagreements are minimized, which brings the Lord's blessing (see Psalm 133:1). For a church to function properly, it must operate with *one mind*, in the *same love, united in spirit,* intent on *one purpose*, and striving *together*. When a congregation thinks alike, it becomes unified. Strife ceases because they move together in the same direction. But if members fight against the shepherd's vision and the direction he's leading, it brings the church to a grinding halt and can even rip it apart.

Vision originates in the mind of God, who then imparts it to godly leaders in step with His Spirit. With it, the church flourishes; without it, it dies. "Where there is no vision, the people perish" (Prov. 29:18). Too often, churches that have lost vision will persecute the pastor who shares his ideas and dreams about the future.

When Joseph in the Old Testament shared his God-given dreams about the future with his brothers, they were filled with rage and sold him into slavery. This set a precedent for all antagonists when the shepherd begins sharing the Lord's vision for the church. A Baptist pastor told us that when he tried to start a new ministry in his church, a deacon went to him privately and vented, "I hate you!"[30]

That shouldn't surprise us. Vision will either unite or divide. It unites those who catch the vision of what God wants to accomplish, but it also infuriates those with an opposing mindset. If the controllers don't embrace God's vision for the church, they'll keep fighting until

---

[30] This pastor was later forced out of his church and is currently working a secular job.

you change course, or they'll get rid of you. A terminated pastor told us, "They were angry, but not because I acted unkind toward them. I just believed what God had put in my heart—a different direction, a new vision, and a different focus than what they had."

Think of a church's vision as a bus traveling toward a destination. You're the driver and the members are your passengers. You're in St. Louis, prepared for a trip northeast to New York. After the bus leaves, a small group of passengers starts protesting, insisting that you take them west to Los Angeles. You think, *Everyone knew this bus was headed to the Big Apple, so why are they demanding to go in the opposite direction now?*

This illustrates what happens when churches have two visions; they lead in opposite directions, causing a split. Division is caused by two visions, and only one can rule a church. God is not the author of confusion (1 Cor. 14:33). One comes from Him, the other doesn't.

If your church is divided over contemporary and traditional music, a blended service where hymns and praise songs are mixed together usually won't please either side. Instead, you might consider having two services; one contemporary and the other traditional, with the same sermon in each.

If you prefer a traditional form of worship, don't apply to a church that is contemporary. Likewise, if you are a potential candidate for a church that's traditional, and you believe contemporary is more appealing, you're probably interviewing with the wrong church—unless they've agreed to the contemporary change you envision. It would be wise to get it in writing.

Don't kid yourself. Music preference is one of the primary causes of church splits. Ministers of music and worship pastors often find themselves in the line of fire when they try to incorporate contemporary songs to the worship, citing "sing to the Lord a new song" (Psalm 149:1). A United Methodist minister shared what happened when the contemporary service outgrew the traditional service.

> As the praise service kept growing in attendance, the traditional service dwindled in numbers. The older crowd became upset and wanted to shut down the praise and worship service. The same small faction made it known they wanted none of "that music of blasphemy" and went out of their way to malign anything associated with growth, change, or for that matter a movement of God.

When you interview with a church, be very clear about your vision and where you plan to take them. Be honest with the search committee. Let them know up front if you'll examine and possibly replace dead programs with new ministries and if you prefer contemporary worship. Make sure they're on the same page with you, with the same mindset, wanting to go in the same direction.

Take a close look at the "bus" too. Some churches have flat tires, no gas, dirty windows, broken engines and dozens of other problems that keep them from leaving the parking lot. And some members want to keep it that way! Some buses are fueled and ready to go, but a few passengers will prevent it from moving forward out of the lot.

Some pastor search committees have been known to tell candidates what they want to hear simply because they need a bus driver. He gladly accepts their invitation, thinking they share the same vision. Then, when God's vision is caught and change begins to occur, they renege on their initial statements and promises.

One prospective pastor clearly explained to the search committee the changes he might make if he were called. The committee members heartily approved his ideas and hired him. Six months after his installation, he began implementing the needed changes as they had agreed. Much to his surprise, some of those same individuals who endorsed his vision suddenly erupted in protest. When he reminded them of their verbal agreement, they claimed they didn't recall making that promise. His mistake was not recording his vision on paper and requiring their signatures.

You can alleviate a lot of misunderstanding if you'll have the church representatives sign an agreement of your vision before you accept a call. Remember, existing programs have a way of becoming sacred cows in some churches, and even if it's a dead cow, they'll refuse to quit worshipping it.

On the other hand, if you're in a church that's willing to follow you, clearly spell out your dreams and keep sharing them. The congregation needs to catch your vision before the antagonists grab the steering wheel to divert it in a different direction. Unless you have the majority of passengers vocally supporting you, those who oppose you will boot you off the bus and leave you stranded.

5. Doctrinal Disagreements

A conflict in theological beliefs can also be a cause for pastor abuse. It's wise to "agree to disagree" on minor doctrinal differences and maintain the unity of the faith. Christians shouldn't fight about their differing views of Bible prophecy and end times, for example. However, we cannot deny the essential truths that are foundational to Christianity.

A mainline denominational pastor told us:

> A group of church members banded together to fight me because I preached that the Bible is God's Word and Jesus is the only way to heaven. They took a more liberal view of the Bible and believed that people of other religions will also go to heaven. It became a heated issue in our church and some members who claimed that Jesus is the only Savior ultimately sided with their friends who believed otherwise. One man who opposed my stance called me "a piece of excrement" although he used another word instead. When I saw that I couldn't change their minds, I resigned as pastor.

As we've said, every church should give liberty to disagree on minor issues, but we can't compromise the foundational tenets of the faith. Paul continually reminded pastors to cling to sound doctrine:

> In pointing out these things to the brethren, you will be a good servant of Christ Jesus, constantly nourished on the words of the faith and of the *sound doctrine* which you have been following (1 Tim. 4:6).

> For the time will come when they will not endure *sound doctrine*; but wanting to have their ears tickled, they will accumulate for themselves teachers in accordance to their own desires (2 Tim. 4:3).

> Holding fast the faithful word which is in accordance with the teaching, that he may be able both to exhort in *sound doctrine* and to refute those who contradict (Titus 1:9).

> But as for you, speak the things which are fitting for *sound doctrine*" (Titus 2:1).

When doctrinal disagreement creates so much friction that ministry becomes impossible, and if you can't remove the abusers, it may be better to leave and start a new church. We'll examine this idea in the final chapter.

6. Inflated Egos

The Pharisees loved the recognition they received from the respectful greetings in the market places and being honored in their synagogues, which inflated their egos. Jesus rebuked them, saying, "Woe to you Pharisees! For you love the front seats in the synagogues, and the respectful greetings in the market places" (Luke 11:43).

An inflated religious ego can be a trap for clergy and laymen alike. Pastors with inflated egos will manipulate their flock through a dictatorial style of leadership, which can be a legitimate reason to terminate a clergyman. However, many pastors are falsely accused of being dictators by defiant congregants. Because the abusers refuse to submit to their shepherd, they must paint him as a tyrant to justify their rebellion.

In so many cases, it's not the pastors with the dictatorial spirit, but the pastor abusers. They are obsessed with being recognized and their entire self-esteem is derived from their status in the church.

Just as the Pharisees loved their religious identity, some folks today bask in the limelight of admiration. Instead of humbly serving to please the Lord, they are secretly motivated by praise and applause from their peers. Phrases like these inflate their ego:

"He's the backbone of this church."
"She's just a saint."
"I don't know where this church would be without him."
"There's no finer person that I can think of than (name)."

In all honesty, it's hard for them to be humble after they've been elevated to sainthood within their church. The recognition they receive becomes the drug for their self-esteem, which makes them desperate to be the center of attention. As with all inflated egos, jealousy enters the picture, ready to attack anyone who might look more attractive.

Abusers are often controlled by the spirit of jealousy, viewing their pastor as the competition. If the pastor starts attracting a large following, they'll start a campaign to ridicule everything he says. It shouldn't surprise us that this tactic isn't new either. "But when the Jews saw the crowds, they were *filled with jealousy*, and began contradicting the things spoken by Paul, and were blaspheming" (Acts 13:45).

Now you understand why they want you gone. It's not ethical or right, but it's certainly real. The way you respond to their attacks will determine the direction of your future ministry. You'll need to learn how to turn the other cheek, while at the same time holding your position of authority.

In the next chapter, I'll list seven signs that indicate trouble may be brewing in your church.

Chapter 4

Signs of Impending Trouble

"And in the morning (you say), 'There will be a storm today, for the sky is red and threatening.' Do you know how to discern the appearance of the sky, but cannot discern the signs of the times?" (Matt. 16:3)

During the first night in our newly built house, my wife and I were soundly asleep when we were suddenly awakened by the piercing shrill of our fire alarm. I quickly leaped out of bed with hands over my ears, and raced toward the blood curdling scream, not knowing what I would find. In the midst of the chaos it dawned on me—I had forgotten to buy a fire extinguisher! Fortunately, it was only a false alarm. But it made me realize that responding to the alarm wasn't enough. I also needed to be prepared to put out the fire.[31]

Imagine how convenient it would be if you could purchase a "trouble alarm" for your church. Although such a handy device is not available, you can look for certain indicators that an "arsonist" in your church intends to start a fire. The warning signs are there, if you will look for them. Jesus said, "You shall know them by their fruits" (Matt. 7:16).

Dealing with troublemakers has to be one of the great paradoxes of ministry. Our congregations are an odd mixture of gentle saints who serve the Lord with gladness, and vicious wolves that are intent on ripping the shepherd apart. With one hand we're feeding the flock, and with the other we're fighting off wolves. We're like Nehemiah rebuilding the wall; "with one hand doing the work and the other holding a weapon" (Neh. 4:17).

What makes it even more confusing is the wolves are dressed like sheep, making us look insensitive and uncaring toward members of the flock. Regardless of how diplomatically we pastors handle these misfits,

---

[31] Pastor Mike Johnston

we invariably come off looking like the bullies instead of them. Nevertheless, that shouldn't deter us from standing up to them.

In his book, *Musical Pulpits*, Rodney Crowell surveyed 386 Protestant pastors who had been forced out of their churches. Typically, the ministers were male, age 47, had been in the ministry for 19 years, and held a Master's Degree.[32] His findings reveal that neither age, longevity, or training are adequate in preparing us for the pastor haters. The solution is to recognize the warning signs and extinguish the fire before it gets out of hand.

Below are seven smoke signals, which indicate that a malicious pyromaniac in your congregation has kindled a fire. If you're going to survive in ministry, you must learn how to investigate cases of spiritual arson before it's too late. The quicker you respond to the alarm, the more likely you'll keep the flame from turning into an inferno.

Sign 1. When you sense in your spirit that something is wrong.

A news segment on television demonstrated how fish are inspected. The most precise way to examine them isn't with technology but with a trained human nose. The inspector smells each part of the fish, trying to detect unusual odors. When a portion smells a bit fishy, it indicates something has gone bad.

Discernment is a gift from God that allows you to detect when something in your church smells fishy. It isn't something you have to hunt for, but when it surfaces, you instinctively know something's wrong. If you sense in your spirit that something is going on behind the scenes, it's probably the Holy Spirit giving you a warning.

Perhaps you sense tension in your church. You don't have any solid evidence, but you can feel it. In most instances, it's likely you are right. Too many of us have a tendency to dismiss our suspicions until it's too late. If you'll talk to those who seem edgy and ask if anything is wrong, you might prevent a fire before it gets started.

Maybe you have an uneasy feeling about a particular person in the congregation. Don't ignore your intuition. Although everyone can misjudge at times, it may be that God is disturbing your spirit so you can avert a larger problem.

If you keep having nagging impressions about a certain situation or person, chances are God is imparting insight you should not ignore.

---

[32] Crowell, Rodney J. *Musical Pulpits.* Grand Rapids, MI: Baker Publishing House 1992, 107-108.

When the Lord leads, He instills peace in your heart that surpasses all understanding. A lack of peace can be a sign of warning that His will is not being followed and something needs to change.

You can also sense if trouble is brewing behind the scenes. One pastor regrets having ignored the impressions God placed on his heart:

> The warning signals began but I didn't recognize them. One of our deacons resigned from the board for flimsy reasons. The widow of a beloved former pastor and her family stopped attending. Then came the drop in giving. Tensions grew . . . [When] I announced my resignation from the pulpit, the deacon who had resigned grinned broadly at me. I had lasted three-and-a-half years.[33]

Although every church experiences conflict, quarrels can be warded off if the correct spiritual action is taken immediately. American Management Association's Florence Stone writes: "Conflicts don't arise without cause, and they usually don't disappear until the cause is addressed. If a conflict isn't resolved, or at least its effects tempered, the conflict's effects can grow."[34]

God knows what trouble brews on the horizon and will let you know through discernment. Don't ignore the signals. If you do, it's at your own peril.

Sign 2. When you start receiving critical emails and threatening phone calls.

When pastors receive kind notes of thanks from laypersons, it lifts them up and energizes them in ministry. God's Word verifies the powerful impact of encouragement when it says, "How delightful is a timely word!" (Prov. 15:23).

Hate mail, on the other hand, has a far more devastating impact; sending clergy into prolonged bouts of discouragement and despondency. Not surprisingly, pastor abusers are actively involved in writing accusatory, angry letters, with the shepherd as the recipient.

Scriptures will likely be cited and words painstakingly chosen to give the impression that the memorandum comes from God's prophet, sent to correct a wayward pastor. If you happen to receive one of these

---

[33] Crowell, 32-33.
[34] Stone, Florence M. *How To Resolve Conflicts at Work.* New York, NY: AMA Publications 1999, 5.

pseudepigrapha, remember that Satan has a master's degree in *trickonometry*, and knows how to cleverly quote Scripture.

Sanballat and Geshem the Arab wrote five letters to Nehemiah, trying to discourage him from completing the wall the Lord had called him to rebuild:

> Sanballat and Geshem sent a message to me, saying, "Come, let us meet together at Chephirim in the plain of Ono." But they were planning to harm me . . . And *they sent messages to me four times in this manner* . . . Then Sanballat sent his servant to me in the same manner *a fifth time with an open letter* in his hand. In it was written, "It is reported among the nations, and Gashmu says, that you and the Jews are planning to rebel; therefore you are rebuilding the wall. And you are to be their king, according to these reports . . . Then I sent a message to him saying, "Such things as you are saying have not been done, but you are inventing them in your own mind." For all of them were trying to frighten us, thinking, "*They will become discouraged* with the work and it will not be done." (Neh. 6:2, 4-6, 8-9)

Like Sanballet and Geshem, pastor abusers often try to discourage God's work by sending threatening messages to pastors. A Mennonite Brethren pastor from Kansas told us he received anonymous letters telling him to leave the church and phone calls at night from strangers, threatening harm to him and his family. A Methodist pastor said, "I received at least a hundred phone calls to my home with silence on the other end."

A pastor in Massachusetts told us, "I started getting obscene phone calls in the middle of the night. They would curse me out, or sometimes they would just be silent on the other end. I received hate mail, cursing me and telling me to go to hell. I would get letters in my box telling me that I was a terrible pastor and that I needed to leave."

As we've said before, pastor abusers truly believe they are following God's instructions and will even boast that their threatening memos are divinely inspired. A Disciples of Christ pastor showed us an eighteen-page letter of grievances against him that an angry man had written and distributed to his congregation. The antagonist wrote: "I am the sole author and responsible for its content on paper, but the real author is the Holy Spirit."

What utter nonsense. How do these critical false prophets get into churches in the first place? Is no one watching the door? Not only are they allowed in, but are often promoted to seats of power. And their attacks against pastors usually begin by getting out a pen and paper.

Their discouraging messages are delivered in a variety of ways—as an email, text, or a typewritten letter. Sometimes they're slipped under your office door in a sealed envelope, waiting to greet you the first thing Monday morning. They can also come in the mail, or secretly left in your box at the church office. Often the messages are unsigned, leaving you wondering who has the vendetta against you.

Your adversary might even deliver the message in a sinister way, without using an envelope. When one pastor and family returned from their vacation, they pulled into their driveway, only to find a two-page hate letter conveniently taped to their front door, flapping in the wind for everyone to read! It had been taped to the door for over a week.

After the abuser has vehemently bludgeoned you to death line by line, he'll often end his hypocritical letter saying, "remember that I love you in Christ." That's like an axe-murderer throwing his victim a Band-Aid. He's compelled to sign his note like that to justify his evilness and to make it sound like you're the problem, not him.

What should you do before opening your hate mail? First, understand that this is spiritual warfare and must be approached using wisdom. This person most likely has a problem with you because he's motivated by an evil spirit. Next, pray that the Lord will protect your heart from being wounded or turning bitter. Finally, remember that the message might contain a grain of truth you need to hear, even though everything else is clearly intended to dismantle you. Ask the Lord to reveal what is a valid concern and what is clearly malicious slander.

Should you answer the letter? Perhaps the best approach is to verbally tell the individual you received the note and let it go at that. Remember, anything you put in writing can *and will* be used against you.

Instead of allowing the hateful message to dishearten you, keep in mind the promise of our Lord, "Blessed are those who have been persecuted for the sake of righteousness, for theirs is the kingdom of heaven" (Matt. 5:10).

Sign 3. When gossip about you starts circulating around the church.

Someone has said that it's impossible to stay ahead of a liar, and if you've ever been slandered, you know just how true this really is. "The lips of the righteous bring forth what is acceptable, but the mouth of the wicked, what is perverted" (Prov. 10:32). A terminated pastor in Tennessee told us:

> Gossip will kill your church. Our church leadership never dealt with the gossipers head on. The elders always encouraged people to come to them with complaints, but they never encouraged those same people to come directly to me to work it out.
>
> One angry lady had been gossiping about me, trying to get me fired. I told her, "If you can't submit to the spiritual authorities in this church, then you need to find a church where you can." That's exactly the way I said it. She went around slandering me to everyone in the congregation, saying that I had told her to get out of the church. "If you don't like what the pastor doing, he will kick you out of the church too!" It wasn't true, but people believed her.
>
> On another occasion, a person who was upset with me told a lie to the elders about my wife. The elders called her in for questioning. The accusation was such an off-the-wall lie that my wife thought they were joking at first. She asked them, "Who told you that I said that?" They said, "We can't tell you. We have to protect the informant's identity."
>
> Now, that's really fair, isn't it? You serve in churches for 21 years, and you get to the point where you're done with it. Church is supposed to be about loving one another and so I told my wife, "I'm not fighting this stuff anymore."
>
> If I had to do it all over again, if I heard anyone say anything about me, I would march over to their house and I would get nose to nose with that person, and in a loving way try to work through the complaint against me. Now, that might not work, but I would serve notice from the get-go, "If I hear of you talking to other people about me again, then I'm going to be on your doorstep again."

As all pastors are keenly aware; the longer gossip is repeated, the more it is believed. We cannot emphasize this enough; when you begin hearing of gossip being spread about you, don't shrug it off. Rumors and negative reports can be the most difficult tactics to stop. If you don't deal with the slander quickly and head on, the next accusation may be of a sexual nature, which would ruin your ministry.

The agents of Satan who start these treacherous rumors are driven by a sense of duty to bring you down. They'll attack you with tenacity and persistence because they operate under a different spirit than you. "A worthless man digs up evil, while his words are as a scorching fire.

A perverse man spreads strife, and a slanderer separates intimate friends" (Prov. 16:27-28)

God gave clear instructions to keep pastors from being unjustly maligned: "Do not receive an accusation against an elder except on the basis of two or three witnesses." (1 Tim. 5:19). Remember this passage whenever *you* hear of derogatory stories being tossed around about your pastor brethren. If you hear malicious gossip about a fellow pastor, resist the temptation to make a judgment based on third-hand reports that can't be substantiated. Never forget that gossip spread through loose-tongued church-goers is one of Satan's crafty devices to destroy God's servants.

Sign 4. When you hear of secret meetings being held without informing you.

Satan's cunning scheme to get rid of the pastor usually involves calling a meeting of his willing accomplices behind closed doors. In that private room, the devious plot to destroy the shepherd is meticulously hashed out. Although the devil is invisible to those gathered, he's aggressively planting sinister thoughts in their minds. Secrecy is of utmost importance, because once the conspiracy is unleashed, it catches the unsuspecting pastor off guard and blindsides him. A former pastor told us:

> The older, wealthy members got together and started having secret meetings. Of course, they didn't bother to tell me about them. I would get word that they had been meeting. When they started withholding their offerings, the elders started meeting with them, trying to get them to not leave the church. They said, "We'll stay on one condition—if the pastor is fired."
>
> Later I heard rumblings again concerning the closest friends of the elders. They had another secret meeting and it turned out that two of my elders were part of it. I came home and told my wife, "The writing is on the wall. We're not going to survive this."

When a pastor in Illinois found out that a secret meeting was being held, he decided to show up unannounced.

> I took a group on a mission trip to Ecuador. When I got back, the leadership team wanted me to decide whether I wanted to keep being pastor of that church. I had only been there fourteen months. I said, "I

would like to see if we can work this out. I would like to remain here."

On the following Monday, I found out the leadership team was having a secret meeting that I was not told about. To their surprise, I showed up at the meeting. I said, "What's going here isn't right. You should not be meeting behind my back. Our conversations need to be face-to-face so we can work this out."

They said, "There's nothing to work out. We've decided we want your resignation."

I told them, "I'm not giving you my resignation. Most of the people in this church love us and they love what's going on here. The church is growing and good things are happening. I'm not going to resign."

They said, "You either give us your resignation or we will screw you professionally." Those were their exact words.

When I didn't resign, it still didn't stop them. A few days later, I was stunned to find out they had written a letter to everyone in the church and told them that I had quit.

The purpose of these secret meetings is to build a case against the pastor when he isn't present to defend himself. Those who are gathered get caught up in a feeding frenzy, as flimsy evidence is presented and truth is ignored. A pastor explained how two deacons instigated a lynch mob by slandering him in a secret meeting:

I found out that two deacons, who were trying to take control of the church, had been calling secret meetings to get rid of me because so many new people were joining. A member, who supported me, informed me that the two deacons convinced the others in their secret meetings that I was being "mean" to people and they would push for my termination.

I asked who these people were that I had supposedly offended. He had a blank stare on his face and said, "You know, they never actually mentioned any names." I told him, "Of course they didn't because they are making it up."

Satan loves to plot evil schemes under the dark veil of secrecy against God's messengers. Something's terribly wrong when a tiny group of antagonists can hold underground meetings to get rid of their pastor. It's just too easy for these thugs to concoct stories or exaggerate incidents to discredit the pastor's ministry and ruin his reputation.

The devil is unmistakably the instigator of secret plots. Nowhere in the Bible do we read about God calling for His people to meet secretly and plot the ousting a pastor. Instead, every instance in the New Testament of plots and secret meetings pertains to ungodly religious leaders who attacked God's Son and His followers.[35]

Jesus said, "I have spoken openly to the world; I always taught in synagogues, and in the temple, where all the Jews come together; and *I spoke nothing in secret*" (John 18:20). So, when you hear of secret meetings, you know it isn't God who is calling them.

How can a church board handle a legitimate concern without a secret meeting? Simply by letting the pastor know about the meeting ahead of time. We heard about a very compassionate pastor who was above reproach in all things, but new people weren't joining the church. Over a period of time, worship attendance declined to the point where the church would have to close its doors if something didn't turn around.

The elders, who greatly loved their pastor, needed to decide whether to find another minister who could grow their congregation, or continue to let the church dwindle. Instead of calling a secret meeting, the board asked the pastor's permission if they could meet to evaluate his job performance. The pastor understood the dilemma and graciously gave them permission to meet.

Although we don't know the end of the story, we commend the church leaders for handling this situation correctly; with submission and respect for their pastor. If they eventually decide to let the pastor go and offer him a severance package, this would certainly not be a case of pastor abuse.

Unfortunately, abusers don't operate in this way because they don't love their pastors. Hence, they will continue to hold secret gatherings to plot his firing.

What can a pastor do if he hears of subversive meetings? When evil men secretly plotted against David, he cried out to God for protection.

> Hide me from the secret plots of the wicked, from the rebellion of the workers of iniquity, who sharpen their tongue like a sword, and bend their bows to shoot their arrows—bitter words, that they may shoot in secret at the blameless. Suddenly they shoot at him and do not fear. They encourage themselves in an evil matter. They talk of laying snares secretly. They say, "Who will see them?" They

---

[35] See Matt. 26:59-60, Acts 6:9-13, 9:23-24, 23:12-13.

devise iniquities: "We have perfected a shrewd scheme." (Ps. 64:2-6 NKJV)

Remember, if you hear of secret meetings and you're not invited, you can be assured that the smoke alarm has been triggered, so you better take action.

Sign 5. When money is used as a tool to manipulate you.
Money manipulation is a clear sign you're being exploited. Sometimes wealthy members will use extortion to coerce ministers into following their instructions instead of God's. They will often threaten to withhold their offerings unless they get their way. Others let the pastor know how much they give to influence him to do what they want. These "offerings" are used as malicious threats and manipulative bribes instead of loving sacrifices to the Lord. Boards will freeze salaries, or if necessary, cut off the pastor's livelihood completely by firing him. A pastor in Florida told us:

> The power bloc who opposed me stopped giving their tithes because they were trying to starve me out, saying the church couldn't afford to keep me. I didn't want to resign. My wife and I were willing to cut our annual income nearly in half and move into a trailer house so that we could stay, because we believed in the vision God had given us for the church. But, some of them didn't want to change. Just as Jesus said, it was like pouring new wine into old wineskins. Eventually they succeeded in forcing me out.

Here's another testimony about a pastor we'll call "Eddie." Eddie had been out of seminary for several years when a rural church in Oklahoma called him to be their pastor. A host of wealthy farmers attended the church, and the deacons prided themselves on the fact that the church designated an enormous portion of their budget to missions. This gave them the unique distinction of being the state leader in percentage missions giving in their denomination.

You would assume that a church with such a heart for missions would also take care of their main missionary, their pastor. Not so in this church. Eddie's take-home pay was so meager he could barely support his wife and two children. When his daughter needed new shoes, he couldn't afford to pay for them. Instead of the church offering assistance, his non-Christian neighbor who felt sorry for him purchased them for her.

Pastor Eddie soon learned that the church operated by a strict "out by twelve o'clock" schedule. The controllers were becoming increasingly upset because he had been preaching past noon. They complained about not seeing the football kickoff on television. Others were unhappy that the other churches in town beat them to their favorite restaurant, forcing them to wait at the back of the line. Eddie believed that preaching God's Word was of utmost importance and that if he went a little past noon, they should understand.

They didn't. In a childish display of rebellious unity, the kingpins actually synchronized their watches so the alarms would beep together exactly at noon. The first Sunday it happened, Eddie chuckled, as did the rest of the congregation. However, it wasn't a laughing matter when they continued to do it every Sunday from then on. The "lunch bunch" became a little more irate each week when he didn't dismiss them on time. Not long afterward they cut him from the church payroll.

Make no mistake about it, pastor abusers' favorite sign is the dollar sign. And it's also another sign that a fire is burning in your church.

Sign 6. When friends turn against you for no apparent reason.
Nothing hurts worse than betrayal from an intimate friend. David recorded the sting of a companion's disloyalty when he wrote: "Even my close friend, in whom I trusted, who ate my bread, has lifted up his heel against me" (Ps. 41:9). Betrayal seems to be a common thread in pastor abuse testimonies. A terminated pastor said:

> It blew me away when a trusted friend and his wife started attacking me for no clear reason. I can only conclude that the hateful group must have slandered me and made up some lies, which they believed. It still puzzles me to this day.

Another pastor shared how he and his wife were betrayed by a close friend of many years.

> Honestly, we thought she would defend us against those who hated us, when in reality they had recruited her as their star witness to denigrate us. I wondered what would make her turn against me. It just didn't make sense. I had coached her family through numerous crisis situations, including rescuing her backslidden daughter from sin. When Martha required an operation, I was in the hospital offering

comfort and prayer, as they wheeled her away on the gurney. I interceded on her behalf and shared Scripture with her and her husband when they called as late as two in the morning. And then, for some unknown reason, she became a part of the anti-pastor faction. What changed her thinking? I found out later that a malicious gossiper fabricated some lies about me. She foolishly accepted the misinformation as the truth.

You don't have to be in the ministry for long before you're the victim of disloyalty. The abusers will often approach your friends, trying to persuade them to come over to their side. They'll misrepresent the situation, distort the facts, and say, "Let us tell you *our* side of the story." If your friend is gullible or has a weak backbone, he or she will cave in to their exploitation, instead of standing up for what's right. It's worth repeating—never underestimate the incredible power of a slanderer to alter people's thinking.

If the devil used a betrayer to get Jesus nailed to the cross, don't be surprised if it happens to you as well. "For you have been called for this purpose, since Christ also suffered for you, leaving you an example for you to follow in His steps" (1 Pet. 2:21).

Don't ignore betrayal as an important sign of impending trouble.

Sign 7. When a spokesperson claims to represent an angry group. Pastor abusers usually rally behind a spokesperson, who finds great satisfaction in orchestrating the attack. His strategy for running off the pastor can be traced back to Absalom, who stood at the city gate, sympathized with every complainer, and "stole the hearts of the men of Israel." Then, he stirred up a rebellion throughout Israel, had them proclaim him as their new leader, and forced King David from this throne (see 1 Chron. 15:2-14). Not surprisingly, this same evil scenario still operates in our churches today.

The Bible warns that "A worthless person, a wicked man, is the one who walks with a false mouth, who winks with his eyes, who signals with his feet, who points with his fingers; who with perversity in his heart devises evil continually, who spreads strife" (Prov. 6:12-14). When a prominent person in your church becomes a spokesperson for dissention, the smoke detector has just activated its high-pitched alarm.

A pastor shared one of the many threats he received in his abusive church:

One of the leaders said, "I've been sent to tell you that if you packed up and left the house tonight, no one would ask questions. We would hate for anything to happen to your wife, your children, or you. It would be a disaster if somebody got hurt."

No one can understand the agony God's shepherds suffer at the hands of these self-proclaimed church bosses except other pastors. No matter what concessions you agree to, you can't make them happy. It's no secret that these bullies typically don't desire unity, but demand compliance with their wishes. They show up at the most inconvenient times to wear you down with complaints. Instead of investing their time to reach the lost, they spend hours making phone calls and visits to other church members, beating the drum of discord.

A Southern Baptist pastor gave the following account:

The deacon board chairman came to see me one evening. He never called to set up an appointment, but just showed up unannounced clutching his gripe list. The deacon asserted that he represented a "growing" number of disgruntled people who were angry with me, and had appointed him as the liaison of church solidarity.

With seeming delight, he claimed that other members were "flooding" him with concerns about me, although he wouldn't disclose names because he wanted to "protect their identities." I later proved his list was contrived and his alleged "growing" number was actually a small group the deacon had recruited.

Casting gentleness to the wind, the deacon tore into me with outlandish accusations. When I asked what specifically I had done wrong, the deacon sidestepped the issue. He wasn't interested in repairing and restoring fellowship, so I refrained from further discussion. Since I wouldn't bow to his intimidation, the deacon started a false rumor about me. Because of the misery I suffered at the hands of this cruel deacon, I resigned as pastor. I'm currently working at a secular job but still ministering as a layman.

Any of these seven signs may be God's way of alerting you of impending trouble. Remember that the Lord is with you, and He gives your troublemakers this stern warning: "Do not touch My anointed ones, and do My prophets no harm" (Ps. 105:15). God will deal harshly with those who ignore His admonition, so don't take matters into your own hands. Instead, cling to God's promise that He will not allow those who attack you to get off the hook: "I will take vengeance. I will repay those who deserve it" (Heb. 10:30 NLT).

Chapter 5

You Might Be a Pastor Abuser If . . .

I urge you, my friends: watch out for those who cause divisions and upset people's faith and go against the teaching which you have received. Keep away from them! For those who do such things are not serving Christ our Lord, but their own appetites. By their fine words and flattering speech they deceive innocent people. (Rom. 16:17-18, CEV)

A United Methodist pastor tragically took his own life after being verbally attacked by an abusive married couple in his church. We interviewed Mark's widow, who told us what happened:

> After Mark made a minor administrative decision, a certain married couple in our church went ballistic. The husband had a reputation for being an egotistical know-it-all and his wife was also known to be hot-headed and defensive. They disagreed with his decision, so they showed up at his office and unloaded their hostility by shouting and swearing.
> As they were unleashing their attack, a woman accidentally walked into the meeting to give Mark a message. When she saw the couple screaming and cursing at him, she turned around and walked out, afraid to get involved. Two teenagers in the hallway also overheard the couple's yelling and using profanities.
> Mark's father had verbally and physically abused him when he was a child and the couple was calling him the same filthy names. He asked them to leave his office, but they refused. When he couldn't take their screaming anymore, he got up and left through the back door.
> The youth pastor in the parking lot noticed tears streaming down his face and asked what was wrong. Mark said, "I ordered them to leave my office and they wouldn't. The religious people crucified Jesus and now they are crucifying me."
> He then drove to a drug store, bought some over-the-counter pills and took an overdose. I firmly believe the couple's screaming and

cursing gave him a flashback of his childhood abuse and pushed him over the edge.

After the husband and wife found out about him taking his life, they never showed any remorse nor did they ask my forgiveness for their vicious attack on him. Ironically, the husband was head of the Staff Parish Relations Committee which welcomed Mark into the church. He and his wife were the ones who brought him to the town, and they were also the ones who destroyed him.

This heart-breaking testimony shows how callous the pastor abusers can be and the devastating effect they can have on ministers. While abusers often join together as a small group to oppose their shepherd, some work independently. That doesn't make them less threatening. It simply makes them less obvious. Even though they're working alone, they can be just as determined to bring you down.

Identifying Potential Pastor Abusers

Jeff Foxworthy is probably best known for his "You Might Be a Redneck If" jokes. We've come up with our own "You Might Be a Pastor Abuser If" lines to help you identify potential troublemakers in your congregation:

- You might be a pastor abuser if . . . you think his 1% annual salary raise is too much.
- You might be a pastor abuser if . . . you take a stand against him on every issue "to keep the church balanced."
- You might be a pastor abuser if . . . you attend a secret meeting to gripe about the pastor.
- You might be a pastor abuser if . . . you've written a job description for the pastor's wife, even though she's not an employee.
- You might be a pastor abuser if . . . you believe he has the easiest job in the world because he "only works on Sunday."
- You might be a pastor abuser if . . . you think the pastor should be using his vacation time for his mission trip to Africa.
- You might be a pastor abuser if . . . you invite the pastor out to lunch so you can correct him on a point of disagreement.
- You might be a pastor abuser if . . . you're friendly to his face but slander him behind his back.

- You might be a pastor abuser if . . . you're lobbying to be on the pastor search committee even though the current minister hasn't left.

Dozens of pastors were interviewed for this book and what they said is no laughing matter. To help you identify potential troublemakers, we're about to introduce you to six pastor haters: Divisive Dave, Critical Claire, Ruthless Ruth, Controlling Chet, Egghead Ed, and Agenda Andy.

Don't let their fictitious names fool you. Although their names have been changed, the testimonies that you're about to read are actual cases of pastor abusers. They each operate a little differently but they're all united in purpose—to oppose God's leaders of the flock.

#1 The Prior Abuser

A football player that gave his high school coach headaches will give his college coach migraines. History will repeat itself. Someone who has been a pastor abuser at a previous time will be after your head as well. This person has a track record of harassing pastors and trying to force them out of the pulpit.

Divisive Dave

Not long after I started our new church, Dave visited our worship service. A mechanic by trade, he was a heavyset man with a bushy beard and usually wore overalls. When I greeted him after the service, he told me, "You're a lot better than Bird Bath."

"What do you mean?" I asked.

"Bird Bath is Pastor Bath, my previous pastor. You preach a lot better than him."

Being new in the ministry, I accepted his statement as a compliment, when in reality he was belittling his former pastor. I couldn't see the huge red flag being waved right in front of my face.

I later learned Dave was one the heavyweights in a big fight in his previous church. The slugfest resulted in a knockout when the church split and then closed its doors. Ignoring his prior pastor abuse track record, I thought Dave would change his attitude and settle down in our friendly little congregation. I was wrong.

It concerned me that Dave's personality was so abrasive, but a friend of his assured me that I had nothing to worry about. "That's just the way he is—he's gruff on the outside, but deep down he has a good heart."

It didn't take long for Dave to start giving me advice. He claimed to have the gift of "preacher correcting" (find that in Scripture), like a prophet God had sent to keep pastors in line. Whenever I talked with him, he would glower at me over the top of his glasses, like a judge peering at the accused while sentencing him.

Months passed, with Dave constantly complaining and criticizing. I kept waiting for his "good heart" to manifest itself in some way, but it never did. It got to where I couldn't sleep at night, always wondering what Dave was up to next. When I began feeling sharp pains in my stomach, I went to the doctor for testing.

After the results came back, he asked, "Have you been under a lot of stress? You're developing an ulcer." He prescribed some medicine to neutralize the acids, but the real acid causing my upset stomach was Dave.

A dark cloud loomed over every worship service and our church quit growing. Visitors were turned off when the first person they saw upon entering the church was grouchy Dave in his overalls. Please grasp this—just one person was generating such a negative atmosphere in our church it cancelled out every positive thing we were doing.

It finally reached a point where our only option for survival was to do as Proverbs 22:10 instructs: "Drive out the scoffer and contention will go out, even strife and dishonor will cease." It would be risky to ask Dave to leave our church and I feared our entire congregation would disband as a result of our decision.

An elder and I went to his repair shop and politely asked him to find another church to attend. Not surprisingly, Dave didn't take the news kindly. He threw down his mechanic's wrench in a fit of rage and vowed never to return.

When the announcement was made the following Sunday, the response from the congregation surprised me. Everyone was relieved and felt reassured because we finally took action. One member commented, "I was wondering how long it would take to show him the door."

The huge load I was carrying vanished. Immediately the cloud over the services lifted and the church started growing again. It was as if the Lord was waiting for us to deal with the troublemaker before He would bless us.

After Dave left our congregation, he found another church to infiltrate. A year or two later, I received a disturbing phone call from his pastor. "Brother Crockett, this is Pastor Miller. We're having a little problem over here."

"It's Dave, isn't it?"

"Oh man, he just split our church!" he moaned.

"Why didn't you call me to ask about him?"

"I didn't call because he said you were mean to him. He divided our church and so many members have left that we're going to close our doors."

Satan used Dave to shut down two churches and ours would have been the third if we had not taken decisive biblical action. I wasn't surprised to learn he quit attending church, claiming all pastors are hypocrites. Ironically, what kept him out of church in reality kept him from destroying more.

And what happened to our church? I enjoyed the privilege of being their pastor for eighteen wonderful years. During that time the Lord grew our fellowship from fifty to five hundred members and the congregation preserved its joyful and friendly atmosphere. I'm convinced that the church wouldn't have survived if we hadn't exercised church discipline to remove this determined antagonist.

#2 The Fault-Finder

A fault-finder is a layperson who points out everything the pastor is doing wrong and never what he's doing right. A consumer survey revealed that a person who likes a product will tell three other people. But a customer who finds something wrong with a product will complain about it to eleven people.

When these statistics are applied to a congregation, it's not difficult to see how someone who persistently criticizes the pastor can wreak havoc in a church. The abuser's continual complaining about the pastor convinces other members to join in the protest, as he recruits an army of unsatisfied customers. These fault-finders band together with one goal in mind—to drive the minister out of business.

One pastor said this about the abusers in his church:

> No matter what you do, you can't please them. You can change everything you do to suit exactly what they want, but then they'll have a list of ten things that you need to change. Then after you do that,

they'll have ten more. Then the week after that, they'll have ten more. You can never please these people.

This tactic by the enemy isn't new, as Satan has always appointed fault-finders to oppose God's leaders. Moses had to deal with his critics in the wilderness who constantly challenged his leadership. Paul was almost killed by his stone-throwing persecutors, and Jesus was crucified by the gnat-straining Pharisees. Common sense would tell you that the miracles they performed authenticated their ministries, but that didn't dissuade their critics. Ignoring the proof, they kept attacking their innocent targets.

Fault-finders view their place in the Body of Christ as the finger, which points out everyone flaws. These self-appointed judges will ride hobby horse issues while sniffing and snorting like a December sneeze. They'll slither into your church with accolades and compliments, but it won't be long before they're wearing you out with accusations and complaints. Since few people have the guts to stand up to a critic, their nitpicking usually goes unimpeded.

Because these abusers show no mercy toward their pastor, God will not let them receive spiritual insight from the one they're judging. As a result, their needs cannot be met—not because the pastor isn't feeding them, but because they have built a wall around their heart which keeps them from receiving from him. This explains why fault-finders will often say, "I'm not getting anything out of the pastor's sermons... I'm not getting my needs met." They'll never be satisfied as long as they continue to criticize their leaders.

Critical Claire

A Southern Baptist pastor shared this about a bitter woman in his congregation:

> Claire was a church hopper who had a notorious reputation as a backbiter, especially when it came to pastors. When she began attending my church, I became the next target of her criticisms. From the get-go she disapproved of everything I did. It seemed I could do nothing right in her eyes.
>
> One night at Bible study I taught on tithing, which was one of her hot-button issues. She saw this as a direct attack against her and her husband because, as I learned later, they weren't givers. She accused me of teaching about giving just so I would become wealthy, not realizing that my pitiful salary had already been set in the church budget.

After enduring months of her picking me apart, I finally decided to draw a line in the sand. I said, "Claire, if you're unhappy with me, why don't you find another church?"

Her reply hit me like a canon ball in the stomach. "We are—but *not just yet.*" I knew she meant. She wasn't finished with her brutal attacks.

One evening before I spoke at an evangelistic event, she called and tore into me for twenty minutes. I didn't have time to listen to her drivel, just before I was about to minister. I finally had to hang up while she was still talking, which provided the ammunition she wanted. Now she would let everyone in her circuit know how mean-spirited I was.

After this incident her church attendance became sporadic, but she continued to slander me behind the scenes, stirring up turmoil in our congregation. She was even able to turn one of my lifelong friends into an enemy by slandering me. Claire eventually left the church, taking a group of her discontented disciples with her.

#3 The Manipulative Flatterer

Every pastor needs encouragement and God wants you to have supporters who will help you. However, flattery is counterfeit encouragement with a hidden motive—to disarm you. The flatterer is trying to manipulate you because he or she wants something in return. Jude 1:16 says, "These are grumblers, finding fault, following after their own lusts; they speak arrogantly, *flattering people for the sake of gaining an advantage.*"

Be extremely leery of those who take you to nice restaurants and talk about the large sums they contribute to the church, as they offer advice to you. Of course, many rich members have pure motives, and they are not to be feared. The ones to watch out for are those who use their money to manipulate.

When Simon the magician tried to buy spiritual authority with money, Peter rebuked him: "May your silver perish with you, because you thought you could obtain the gift of God with money!" (Acts 8:20)

Those who are the friendliest to you now could become your harshest persecutors later. The sweet talker can quickly turn into a malicious slanderer if you don't bow down to his or her wishes. Kenneth Haugk warns, "Those who lavish effusive, gushing praise on you now will often be equally generous with their criticism later."[36]

---

[36] Haugk, 72.

Ruthless Ruth

I heard that a wealthy woman had caused trouble in a nearby church and then left. After visiting many other churches in town, Ruth and her husband decided to attend one of our services. Afterward she told me, "Rick and I have been rating all the preachers in town from 1 to 10. We give you a 10!" They joined our fellowship, took my wife and me out to dinner several times, and showered us with praise.

All their flattery made me forget about the problems she had caused in her previous congregation. Ruth appeared to be the ideal supporter, so I concluded the other church must have been wrong for not seeing it. I made the mistake of ignoring her previous history.

It's always been my policy to never look at the contributor records. I don't want my attitude toward someone to be swayed by the amount of money they give. But this couple would frequently tell me the generous amount they gave in the offering and then act humble about it saying, "We don't want people to know, so don't tell anyone." (They just wanted *me* to know!)

As months passed, I started hearing reports from a growing number of members that this woman was acting like a bulldozer, running over people and bullying them around. She would make hurtful, sarcastic remarks about individuals she didn't like and openly made fun of unattractive people. This woman was tearing our church apart, one person at a time.

After hearing about the mounting number of people she had wounded from valid sources, I asked her if she would go to those she had offended and apologize.

The next Sunday morning before church, Ruth was visibly upset with me. Puzzled by her anger, I inquired, "What's wrong?"

She wiped a tear from her eye and blurted, "We'll talk about it after church!"

That afternoon I learned something new about how antagonists operate. Although I knew at least ten church members she had hurt by her rude remarks and domineering actions, she expected my undying support of her. After all, she and her husband had taken my wife and me out to dinner on several occasions, and now it was time for me to return the favors.

Although I had previously been naïve, now everything suddenly made sense as I reflected on their flatteries and generosity. Their kindness was a tool to manipulate me, a bribe, so I would protect her callous behavior. Like Jezebel, she wanted to be queen of the church—and I was supposed to play the role of Ahab.[37]

When I refused to endorse her vicious behavior, Ruth became "Ruthless." She turned her fury against me, aligning with another headstrong abuser who had crept into our congregation after causing problems in his previous church. (Troublemakers are immediately drawn to each other like iron to magnets.) Thankfully, our elders took a stand against them and the rebels chose to leave.

Ruth joined another church and used the same tactics to manipulate her way into power. Later, some members of that fellowship shared with me that their pastor told his elders, "Either Ruth leaves or I'm leaving!"

#4 The Control Freak
The Control Freak is the easiest pastor abuser to spot because he or she loves to be visibly in charge of everything. There's no secret here. This individual is swollen with pride and demands that you secure his permission before doing anything.

Control Freaks love to remind you of their importance and are known to let their money do the talking. While Flatterers use gifts to *charm* the pastor, Control Freaks often use their wealth to *pressure* him to do what they want. They like to get their point across by withholding their offerings, freezing the pastor's salary, or threatening him with unemployment. In any other setting but church this is called extortion.

Don't confuse the Control Freak with the Loving Leader. God gives some people the gift of leadership, which will always operate in humility and cooperation. Leaders are ordained of God and fully realize their entrusted stewardship responsibilities. Control Freaks, on the other hand, consider themselves arbiters of truth and the owners of the church, and they'll never cooperate with the pastor.

You won't have a hard time figuring out who they are. Just listen when a decision needs to be made. They'll be the first ones to voice their opinions as the only option.

Controlling Chet
A United Methodist pastor wrote the following testimony about "Chet," who was part of an antagonistic faction that forced him out.

---

[37] See 1 Kings 21.

I met with the Trustees to discuss the need for a new interchangeable sign in front of the church. Our church was located on a busy highway and a new, highly visible sign would be the easiest and most economical way to attract visitors.

After receiving the blessings of the Trustees to move forward on the project, I called a friend in the sign business, who offered to build our new sign at his cost. I praised God even more when I found someone else outside of the church willing to pay for it completely.

As we were setting the sign in its place, Chet came charging up in his pickup truck and literally almost slid his vehicle into the construction crew. Jumping out of his truck with a red face, he slammed the door and hollered at me, "Who do you think you are, putting up this sign? How dare you not go through the protocol to do it?"

Chet was one of our Trustees but had not attended the previous meeting where the sign had been approved. He had been tipped off by a mean-spirited woman in our congregation, who had spread rumors and lies about me on several occasions. In this case, she made it look like I hadn't consulted with the board.

I bit my tongue as he yelled at me for the next fifteen minutes. I calmly explained to him that I had received approval from the Trustees, and then left him with the other three men who tried to convey the truth.

After this, the tide changed throughout the whole church. Our Staff Parish Relations (SPR) Chair accused me of stealing a church credit card and running up a $10,000 debt on it. This was an outrageous lie because the church didn't even have a credit card. Even so, a small faction continued to spread venom about me. Then they ran off the youth director—after 23 youth came to Christ and another 43 joined the church. This antagonistic group did not like to see change in their church, even if God was the one doing it!

Shortly after this, I went out to my driveway and found a tire on my van had been slashed, as had been a tire on my other car. Later that evening, I found that the same person who had done this had gotten under the hood and removed a relay for the headlights. There is no question it had been removed. The relay sits in a box under the hood and there is no possible way for it to come out on its own. This group meant business and was determined to get its way.

Over the course of two years as their pastor, I found my confidence and ministry turned upside down by a handful of hateful individuals that had no desire for real church to happen. As long as the bills were paid and they had a place to come on Sundays to spend with their like-minded friends each week, they were content.

The striking blow of reality came a month after we moved to another church, when Chet bragged to a friend who is still a church member, "Isn't it good to have our church back!"

My question is, "*What* church?" The majority of real saints left when we did and those remaining simply wanted to be in a maintenance mode.

#5 The Know-It-All

While the Control Freak is the most domineering, the Know-It-All appears at first to be the most cooperative. He may begin as your supporter, providing helpful information and offering suggestions. What sets him apart is that he's convinced *he alone* knows best how to run the church. He'll befriend you, but only as long as you're heeding his advice. Marshall Shelley in his book, *Well-Intentioned Dragons,* writes:

> Within the church, they are often sincere, well-meaning saints, but they leave ulcers, strained relationships, and hard feelings in their wake. They don't consider themselves difficult people. Often they are pillars in the community, but for some reason, they undermine the ministry of the church. They are not naturally rebellious or pathological; they are loyal church members, convinced they're serving God, but they wind up doing more harm than good. They can drive pastors crazy—or out of the church.[38]

Egghead Ed

Another Southern Baptist pastor explained how he was forced out by a deacon who thought he knew best how to run the church:

> Ed was chairman of the deacons at our church and was frustrated with his job at an electrical company. He wanted to be a pastor, but since he had been divorced and had no ministerial training, he knew that no church would call him.
>
> Not long after I became their pastor, I found out that after the church's previous pastor resigned, Ed had submitted his own resume to the search committee. A church member told me Ed's feelings were hurt when the committee turned him down and called me as pastor instead.
>
> I met with the deacons every month to discuss church issues. I always got their approval before moving forward, but I could sense that Ed resisted my leadership. Whenever I made a suggestion, he would counter it with a different idea. Because he had been a deacon at the church for a number of years, he had his own ideas about how the church should be run and preferred to keep it as it had always been.

---

[38] Shelley, Marshall. *Well-Intentioned Dragons*. Grand Rapids, MI: Bethany House Publishers, 1985, 11.

Ed never visited other churches, except on special occasions. The totality of his "knowledge" about church came from his own experience in this congregation as a deacon. Ed was completely out of touch with the changes taking place in churches today and couldn't relate to anyone outside his small circle of friends. His ministry philosophy was, "If it's broke, don't fix it."

I believe a church needs to do whatever it takes to win people to Christ and make disciples, which might mean trying new methods. I've been a pastor for many years and have attended numerous church conferences and seminars. I've learned that if people dread attending a particular program and the attendance keeps dwindling, then it's probably time to start a different ministry that's meeting real needs. Ed would take the opposite approach and make people feel guilty for not supporting the unpopular program.

A year after my arrival, the Lord began blessing in incredible ways. New people were joining the church, many had been saved and baptized, and worship attendance jumped forty percent. Sunday school enrollment skyrocketed and the services were filled with excitement. Ed didn't join in the enthusiasm. He never smiled, nor did he ever speak a word of encouragement or appreciation to me. It bothered him that so many new people were joining the church. He and his buddies were being outnumbered!

One evening I was shopping in the mall with my wife and I happened to run into a deacon's wife. "Where's Paul tonight?" I asked. "Oh, he's at a deacon's meeting at our house. Didn't you know about it?"

Why would the deacons have a meeting at someone's house and not let me know? I wondered. All the other meetings had been at the conference room at church.

Ed had called this secret meeting of all deacons without informing me. I didn't know that this get-together was to discuss getting rid of me. Even though the church was in revival, Ed and a couple of his deacon buddies were angry. They didn't like all the new people joining the church, which was changing the look of the congregation.

At the next scheduled deacons meeting at the church, I knew something was wrong when the inactive deacons also showed up. Some of these guys rarely attended church, maybe twice a year, but came to this meeting to show their solidarity with Ed. I sat there helpless as they verbally attacked me for the next two hours. Most of these deacons had supported me until Ed had his secret meeting with them. Apparently Ed must have said something to smear my character, enough to get them to withdraw support of me.

"Aren't you guys excited about what the Lord is doing here?" I asked. "People are getting saved and joining the church. This church could reach thousands for Christ."

"We don't care about that!" yelled one deacon.

It stunned me that the deacons didn't care about reaching the lost! Nevertheless, I told them I would do whatever I could to keep peace and offered to take each deacon to lunch to listen to them individually. Before I had time to make my first luncheon appointment, Ed called another secret meeting of the deacons. He had compiled a long list of ridiculous demands that I must follow or be fired.

Although I had support from nearly eighty-five percent of my congregation, I knew it wouldn't be wise to engage in an ugly fight with this bunch. Some of the deacons were related to church members who supported me, but would probably flip sides under pressure. The skirmish would cause tremendous damage to the congregation and I shuddered to think of the toll it would take my wife, who was already emotionally distressed by the deacon attacks. After praying for the Lord's wisdom, I negotiated a severance agreement and resigned as pastor.

After I resigned, nearly all the new members left the church as well. A church member told me that after they formed the next pastor search committee, Ed had again submitted his resume as a candidate to be their pastor.

#6 The Single-Issue Activist

Single-Issue Activists elevate one concern above all else. Their mission progresses from a suggestion, to a cause, to a campaign. What's confusing is that you may even whole-heartedly agree with the worthiness of the cause. However, a problem arises when the issue is placed under the spotlight and turns into the hot topic of the church.

Their focus can be anything; music, missions, a doctrinal position, a social cause, dress code, or you name it. As we've said, these issues might even be correct and important. However, a church can get sidetracked when a concern becomes so magnified that it becomes the focal point above all else. The church, in turn, becomes lopsided and loses its direction and purpose.

Not surprisingly, every issue regardless of its validity will attract an activist to promote it. Some advocates understand their boundaries and know how to interact with others diplomatically. Those who don't understand the big picture will campaign for their cause until it's either adopted or divides the church. This person is "the eye," who wants everyone else in the body to be an eye, and is clueless about how the church must work together.[39]

Agenda Andy

A non-denominational pastor explained how a member of his church continually hounded him:

> Not long after Andy joined our church, he took me out to lunch. During the meal, Andy shared about a foreign missionary friend who needed support, and then moved on to another subject. (I've learned to be nervous about lunch invitations because an agenda is usually involved.)
>
> A couple of weeks later, Andy buttonholed me in the hallway after church and said, "I was just wondering if you had thought any more about my missionary friend."
>
> I hadn't even thought about it since then. "Was I supposed to pray for him?" I asked.
>
> "Actually, I was wondering if our church might want to start supporting him."
>
> "I'm not sure," I explained. "We already support a number of missionaries and our budget is tight at this time."
>
> "Well, I hope you'll change your mind," he replied. "There's nothing more important than missions."
>
> Over the next few months, Andy kept bringing up the missionary's name. I found myself avoiding him because I didn't want to have the same conversation for the umpteenth time. It seemed as if *nothing else going on in the church* was important to him. Although I love missions, I want all giving to be done with a cheerful heart and not as a result of pressure tactics. I felt pressured to give to his cause.
>
> After I told him the church wouldn't be supporting his friend, Andy's demeanor turned. Whenever we met in the hallway, he always wore a scowl on his face. He started voicing his complaints to one of our elders, who was known to lend a sympathetic ear to troublemakers. They quickly became close friends and the activist used the elder as a mouthpiece for his issue. When he still didn't get his way, Andy quit the church. I've got to admit that I was actually relieved when he left.

Did You Recognize Someone?

You've been introduced to several potential pastor abusers, and you might have even recognized a few people. Don't become paranoid, but don't be fooled either. There's too much at stake if you ignore the warnings.

---

[39] See 1 Cor. 12:16-17.

Chapter 6

The Silent Majority

> But we request of you, brethren, that you appreciate those who diligently labor among you, and have charge over you in the Lord and give you instruction, and that you esteem them very highly in love because of their work. (1 Thess. 5:12-13)

When Rosina Hernandez was in college, she attended a rock concert where a young man was brutally beaten, while the crowd did nothing to help him. The next day, horror struck when she read the teen had died as a result of the pounding. She never forgot the incident, and was ashamed of being an apathetic onlooker.

Some years later, Rosina had opportunity to redeem herself. A car driving in the rain ahead of her suddenly skidded and plunged upside down into the Biscayne Bay. Within moments, a woman surfaced begging help for her husband still trapped inside.

This time Rosina waited for no one. She plunged into the water and tried unsuccessfully to open the car door. She then pounded on the back window, but it wouldn't budge. Seeing bystanders watching on the causeway, she screamed at them to help her rescue the man inside the car.

Finally, one man and then another came to help. Together they broke the safety glass and dragged the man out. Their help arrived just in time, for if they had delayed a few more minutes, he would have drowned. After the woman thanked Rosina for rescuing her husband, she had promised herself that she would never again fail to do anything she could to save a human life.[40]

Most pastors could use a person like Rosina when the abusers start attacking. Although the majority of your members are on your side, it won't make any difference if they remain silent when you need them to speak up. Your sympathizers are the friendly members in your

---

[40] Adapted from Bits & Pieces, June 24, 1993, 20-21 as quoted in www.sermonillustrations.com

fellowship who are faithful attendees, hard workers, and have always been kind to you. When things are going well, they'll follow you anywhere. But when the pastor abusers begin their beatings, you'll quickly discover they don't want to get involved. Friends you've prayed with, cared for, and cried with, suddenly become fearful, and without a word back away from you.

An abused pastor told us how heart-broken he felt when the members who supported him but wouldn't take a stand:

> In our congregation of 300 members, there were about 20 to 25 cruel people who resisted my leadership. The other 275 were wonderful, kind people, but they didn't have the courage to speak up in my defense, so I had to deal with them alone.

As difficult as it may be to understand this, sympathy has redefined itself in the church. A "sympathizer" now means someone who supports you "in spirit," but doesn't care enough to speak up in your defense against your assailants. If it's any consolation, remember that no one spoke up for Jesus either:

> And after these things Jesus was walking in Galilee; for He was unwilling to walk in Judea, because the Jews were seeking to kill Him . . . The Jews therefore were seeking Him at the feast, and were saying, "Where is He?" And there was much grumbling among the multitudes concerning Him; some were saying, "He is a good man"; others were saying, "No, on the contrary, He leads the multitude astray." *Yet no one was speaking openly of Him for fear of the Jews.* (John 7:1, 11-13)

Pastor, it would be helpful to recall the words of the Lord Jesus: "Remember the word that I said to you, 'A slave is not greater than his master.' If they persecuted Me, *they will also persecute you*" (John 15:20). Just as evil religious people wanted to destroy Him, so they will do to you. Just as the congregation's opinions were divided over Jesus, so it will be with you. Even as Christ's sympathizers were afraid to speak up, the same will happen to you.

In far too many cases, your sympathizers back down from the bullies, choosing to ignore your predicament. They undoubtedly feel sorry for you, but for some indefensible reason, they don't care enough about their pastor to take a stand against the mutiny. As a result, you'll have to take on the abusers by yourself.

This lack of loyalty is more widespread than you might think. One former pastor that we interviewed moaned:

> The hardest part was that so many people who supported me were silent when I needed them the most. When a critical person would tear into me in a business meeting, no one would come to my defense. After one meeting, a guy told me, "I can't believe he beat you up like that." I replied, "So why didn't you say anything to stop him?" I decided to leave the pastorate because their brutality was too hard on me and my family.

Another terminated pastor told us:

> When I was attacked, I sat back and expected my leadership team to back me and stand with me. And in no situation did they ever do that.

J. B. Simmons in his article "Let's Run Off the Preacher" writes:

> I remember the feeling of aloneness and cutoffness [sic] which came over me when I finally realized my church was throwing me out. Although I knew in my head that the vast majority of my people still loved me, I felt cut off from them because they allowed such a cruel thing to happen.[41]

And yet another pastor shared his feelings of abandonment:

> The entire validity of my ministry had been called into question, and no one said a word in my defense. My best friend had walked out, unwilling to take a stand. I went home and cried.[42]

Why Should the Sheep Protect the Shepherd?

You may be asking yourself, *Isn't it the pastor's role to protect the sheep? Why should the sheep have to protect the shepherd?* That's a valid question. It's because many churches have allowed wolves to seize power. The pastor needs reinforcements to fight off two strategies used by abusers—slanderous accusations and forced termination. If an

---

[41] Simmons, J. B. "Let's Run Off the Preacher" The Baptist Program.
[42] Shelley, 98.

innocent person is falsely accused and put on trial, he will probably be found guilty unless other witnesses come forward and negate the misleading claims.

It's appalling that rebels, who aren't accountable to anyone, are allowed to put God's shepherds on trial for flimsy reasons. Remember, pastors have already been placed under the microscope and qualified for ministry through the ordaining process. And before a pastor is hired by a church, he has been through a background check to make sure he hasn't been in legal trouble, a credit check to find out if he pays his bills on time and doesn't owe anyone, and a reference check to find out about any personal problems he might have.

He has also gone through several interviews and answered numerous questions asked by the pastor search committee. Don't forget that his wife must also find approval in their eyes. Finally, he preaches a sermon to the congregation so they can evaluate his speaking abilities, and then vote on whether they want him to come. Then after he accepts the call to their church, he finds himself still under the microscope, being picked apart by the pastor haters who criticize his every move.

In sharp contrast, no other church member is held to such a high standard as the pastor, or scrutinized as carefully. This double standard allows power-hungry misfits to get a free pass and promote themselves within the congregation. Once these thugs have gained a foothold in the church, they become self-appointed spokespersons for every grievance and will try to work their way into positions of authority.

If the abusers had been kept out of power, it's unlikely the pastor would need protecting. But once the wolf pack has ganged up on the shepherd, the only way they can be fended off is if other leaders and laypersons will speak up. One ex-minister told us, "No pastor can win the war against entrenched antagonists unless the rest of the church will support him."

It stands to reason that if your supporters would display their solidarity, they could put a halt to your unwarranted mistreatment and send a message to the abusers that their rebellion won't be tolerated. Unfortunately, the sympathizers typically don't unite with the same fervor as the anti-pastor faction.

Why won't your supporters stand with you? We've condensed it to seven possible reasons.

Reason #1 Your sympathizers aren't as committed to ministry as you are.

If you're like most pastors, your decision to enter "full-time ministry" came after much consideration and prayer. You chose to take on a much higher level of commitment when you accepted God's call to be a pastor.

After graduating from college, I chose to invest my life and money in three additional years of ministry training in seminary. Everyone in the institution sacrificed something to pursue their callings. While attending school, I worked as a janitor scrubbing toilets and showers on campus, making just enough money to get by. Many of my fellow students had left promising careers in the medical field to become pastors. One of these brothers had been a pharmacist, who quit his job and sold everything to pay for his ministerial education. Another friend had been an electrical engineer.

I'll never forget my first day in chapel when the president of our seminary challenged us to "make sure of your call because sometimes that will be all you'll have to cling to." I didn't realize at the time that his challenge was actually a prophetic warning of the abuse we were all about to experience.

I often wonder if some of my classmates who had walked away from lucrative secular careers ended up in abusive churches, where the pastor haters tormented them and their families. Were they driven from their pulpits and returned to secular jobs? What toll did it take on their innocent wives, who had been faithfully serving the Lord with their husbands? At least they had another career to fall back on, unlike so many pastors who are kicked out of their churches.

Yes, pastor, you've been faithful to the Lord's directive; preparing for ministry, working extra jobs, enduring troublesome people, being grossly underpaid, and serving under difficult circumstances—and most of your congregation will never understand the sacrifice that you've made to be their pastor. More than likely, your dedication to serving the Lord is above and beyond the commitment of most of your congregants.

As a result, when the abusers start attacking, you'll often find yourself standing alone. Like the guy getting mugged at the concert, the bystanders didn't care enough to intervene and stop the beating. Your sympathizers don't want to get involved either, so they'll stand unscathed on the sidelines—cheering you on, at best.

This also happened to Paul. After Alexander the coppersmith abused him, his supporters deserted him, leaving him to cope with the bully alone:

> Alexander the coppersmith did me much harm; the Lord will repay him according to his deeds . . . At my first defense *no one supported me, but all deserted me*; may it not be counted against them. (2 Tim. 4:14,16)

Take special note of Paul's insightful warning, "may it not be counted against them." Those who were too afraid to stand up and judge Alexander's sin would be held accountable on the Judgment Day. That's why pastors need to inform their sympathizers that bigger issues are at stake; protecting the Church of the Lord Jesus and the judgment they'll face for failing to do so.

Reason #2 Your sympathizers have learned to tolerate the pastor abusers.

In the name of "peacemaking" many church members will not confront the troublemakers in their congregations. Because God hates those who spread discord among the brethren, every member must join together to stop it. Unfortunately, we've been programmed in our politically-correct environment to be "tolerant" of everyone, no matter how devilish they may be. This is wrong! The Scriptures tell us otherwise. Our Lord Jesus rebuked the Church at Thyatira for being tolerant of a hell-bent woman named Jezebel:

> "I know your deeds, and your love and faith and service and perseverance, and that your deeds of late are greater than at first. But *I have this against you, that you tolerate the woman Jezebel*, who calls herself a prophetess, and she teaches and leads My bond-servants astray . . ." (Rev. 2:19-20).

What was this church doing wrong? They *tolerated* a self-named "prophetess" and conveniently looked the other way when she started disrupting the fellowship. No doubt many naively shrugged their shoulders and said, "Hey, that's just the way she is." Rather than putting a stop to her anarchy, they enabled her by sticking their heads in the sand as she took over control of the congregation.

Many churches today are similar to Thyatira; doing some good deeds, but tolerating the Jezebels and abusers in the congregation. And, like Thyatira, Jesus says, "I have this against you" because they refuse to confront the evil-doers in their midst. Edmund Burke wisely stated, "All that is necessary for the triumph of evil is that good men do nothing." This saying is personified when idle sympathizers watch the pastor haters mistreat their shepherd.

How do the abusers get away with it time and again, and are never held accountable by anyone in the flock? It's because they're tolerated.

Reason #3 Your sympathizers don't feel the pain you're experiencing.

Although the tactics of your adversaries are clear to you, your sympathizers don't understand what's happening to you behind the scenes. Remember, pastor abusers tend to do most of their attacking out of sight so the rest of the congregation can't see it.

Their fight plan is both sinister and well-orchestrated. They usually don't knock out the pastor with one powerful blow. Instead, they spread out their punishment a little at a time, here and there. It's not as obvious using that technique, and it's the accumulated effect that eventually wears him out and saps his strength. Like a boxer who has been continually punched for nine rounds, he's ready to fall in the tenth. The combined damage of their incessant battering takes its toll, until one final punch brings him down.

Understandably, how *could* your sympathizers truly feel your pain? No one feels the brunt of damage like you do. They're not present to hear the snide remarks that the abusers make to you. They never read the attack letters and emails, or listen in on the berating phone calls in the middle of the night. They don't receive ridiculous orders from the control group. They aren't the victims of slanderous gossip like you are, or threatened with losing their jobs.

After being violated by those who claim to be Christians, you're ashamed to divulge what's happened to you until it's too late for anyone to help. As a result, your supporters don't have a clue about the agony the abusers are putting you through. And if they don't feel your pain, it's unlikely they'll try to stop it.

Reason #4 Your sympathizers don't want to lose their "friends."

Your supporters often have had a relationship with the abusers long before you arrived on the scene. They trust them and consider them friends, even though they've only witnessed their pleasant side. However, if your sympathizers were to become pastors, they would certainly become the recipients of their viciousness, just as you have. But that probably will never happen, so your followers will never taste your adversaries' fury. Their relationship is friendship, not fellowship, which is the reason your backers won't confront your abusers.

While it's wonderful to have friends, fellowship is a higher calling. Friendship proceeds from the soul and is based on emotion, while fellowship proceeds from the spirit and is established on God's kingdom. What passes as "fellowship" in some churches is usually just friendship. It's similar to establishing rapport with an unsaved neighbor or fellow employee—chatting on a regular basis about families and football, but without touching the spiritual realm. On the friendship level, camaraderie is often established between members within your church, without even considering what's best for God's kingdom.

Your supporters understand these antagonists are determined to run you off, and they prefer to stay out of the line of fire when it happens. When the faction begins persecuting you, the depth of your supporters' spiritual walk will determine which position they'll take and which side they'll choose.

But remember, their loyalty to their friends can overrule sound judgment, and in this case probably will. Because they've known the pastor-haters for so long, it's going to be difficult to cut off their relationship with them (even though it's an unhealthy one). Since your passion to further God's kingdom isn't their highest priority, they'll choose the abusers' friendship over you.

Besides, they view preachers as temporary and easily replaceable. Pastors come and go every couple of years, but the abusers are permanent and will never leave. So why break off a longtime friendship with a church member to stand up for a pastor that will probably leave anyway?

As they evaluate the situation, they conclude it's less painful for them to lose one preacher than several friends. Face the hard facts, good brother—you're dispensable! They'll just hire another pastor to replace you.

After you're gone, don't be surprised when you hear the wolves aren't being held accountable for destroying you. Much to your chagrin, your supporters will quickly make up with the abusers and learn to get along with them again as if nothing had ever occurred.

Reason #5 Your sympathizers may have been deceived by the abusers.

Do you think the abusers are maintaining a code of Biblical integrity and are speaking kindly about you to your supporters? Of course, not! They're on a mission and have a neatly packaged, slanderous account about how evil you are—and how they're just trying to save the church from your tyranny.

Never underestimate the incredible power of a lie to alter someone's thinking. Anyone can be deceived, no matter how loyal they have been. Those who once enthusiastically supported you may now begin questioning your integrity, simply because slander is such a powerful tool to discredit you. It's startling how quickly some people will believe bad reports without ever examining the facts.

Pastor Mike Johnston said:

> My wife and I were friends with one person for twenty-five years. When I was assaulted, she assured me of her allegiance by quoting a verse: "For where you go, I will go. Your people shall be my people, and your God, my God" (Ruth 1:16). I had no reason to doubt her sincerity.
>
> However, I failed to take into account the *slander factor,* which is the exponential power a phantom allegation proclaimed through an alliance of troublemakers. These particular pastor abusers banded together and fed her misinformation, which she never challenged. Since the accusers kept repeating their lies, it convinced her that they must be telling the truth. Without asking me to respond to their charges, she swallowed the bait, reneged on her promise, and joined their team. After three months of unreturned phone calls, it became painfully evident our lifelong friend wanted nothing more to do with us.

This woman forsook a pastoral friend in my hour of need by willfully choosing to believe lies over the truth. Conspiracy and slander are Satan's favorite weapons in attacking God's messengers, as these Scriptures bear witness:

> **Against Jesus:** Now the chief priests and the whole Council *kept trying to obtain false testimony* against Jesus, in order that they might put Him to death; and they did not find any, even though *many false witnesses came forward.* But later on two came forward (Matt. 26:59-60).

Against Stephen: But some men from what was called the Synagogue of the Freedmen . . . rose up and argued with Stephen. Then *they secretly induced men to say*, "We have heard him (Stephen) speak blasphemous words against Moses and against God." And *they stirred up the people*, the elders and the scribes, and they came upon him and dragged him away, and brought him before the Council. And *they put forward false witnesses* who said, "This man incessantly speaks against this holy place, and the Law" (Acts 6:9, 11-13).

Against Paul: And when it was day, the Jews *formed a conspiracy and bound themselves under an oath*, saying that they would neither eat nor drink until they had killed Paul. And there were more than forty who formed this plot. (Acts 23:12-13).

Since the devil incited corrupt religious leaders against Jesus, Stephen, and Paul, it's likely he'll do the same to you. Secret meetings, devious plots, false witnesses, and character assassination are all powerful weapons in Satan's arsenal, which are cunningly employed to destroy innocent pastors. All he needs is a naïve sympathizer who is willing to listen to the other side.

Reason #6 Your sympathizers are afraid of the abusers and will cave in to their peer pressure.

One of the most vicious wolf attacks on record occurred in New Rockford, North Dakota on March 1888. A pack of wolves tore apart a father and son as the horror stricken wife watched from a window; too frightened to do anything to stop it.[43]

Ezekiel rebuked the ungodly, corrupt leaders of his day, saying, "Israel's officials are like *ferocious wolves*, ripping their victims apart" (Ezek. 22:27 CEV). Jesus said, "Beware of the false prophets, who come to you in sheep's clothing, but inwardly are *ravenous wolves*" (Matt. 7:15). Paul added, "I know that after my departure *savage wolves* will come in among you, not sparing the flock (Acts 20:29).

It's no coincidence that Jesus, Ezekiel, and Paul all characterized them as wolves, and their nature as vicious. No wonder church members feel intimidated by the abusive group and are secretly fearful of them. They don't want to be listed on the wolves' menu either. It's

---

[43] Saint Paul Daily Globe, March 8, 1888, as quoted in www.aws.vcn.com/wolf_attacks_on_humans.html

the same intimidation the Pharisees utilized against anyone who disagreed with them:

> His parents said this because they were *afraid of the Jews*; for the Jews had already agreed, that if anyone should confess Him to be Christ, *he should be put out of the synagogue.* (John 9:22).

Don't overlook the power of peer pressure. No one likes to take a stand alone when an angry group is demanding conformity. It's much easier for your sympathizers to succumb to their hypocrisy than to stand up for you.

To demonstrate the powerful influence of "group think," we find that two pillars of the faith, Peter (Cephas) and Barnabas, caved in to the hypocrisy of the Judaizers, who mixed the Law with grace. Paul rebuked them for being cowards:

> But when Cephas came to Antioch, I opposed him to his face, because he stood condemned. For prior to the coming of certain men from James, he used to eat with the Gentiles; but when they came, he began to withdraw and hold himself aloof, *fearing the party of the circumcision.* And the *rest of the Jews joined him* in hypocrisy, with the result that *even Barnabas was carried away* by their hypocrisy. (Gal. 2:11-13).

If the apostles Peter and Barnabas didn't have enough courage to rebuke the false teachers and stand up for the truth, why do you assume your supporters will do it? Consequently, don't be surprised if those who formerly supported you will try to please both you *and* the lynch mob—depending on whose company they are with at the moment.

Reason #7 Your sympathizers don't understand that eternal souls will be lost if the abusers win.

If you're preaching God's Word and people are being saved, you can expect to be attacked. Nothing can decimate and demoralize an army more than taking out its general. We've heard numerous reports about men of God who were fired (*always* by an angry, powerful group), even though their only "crime" was growing their congregations.

It only makes sense that if you remove the person responsible for the growth, it will stop happening. Consequently, when the pastor is forced out, people who would have been saved through his ministry could wind up in hell. Hence, pastor abuse has eternal consequences, reaching beyond what is observed at the present moment.

Admittedly, in a small church where friendships form before pastors are installed, your supporters may not speak up for you because they don't want to upset their friends. They've seen pastors come and go, but the antagonists remain. It's time to reinforce to your sympathizers that *eternal souls are at stake* and they will answer to God for failing to take godly action. Saving eternal souls is more important than saving temporary friendships.

A Defense Strategy

You would be wise to inform the silent majority as soon as the abuse begins, especially your godly church leaders. Although you might have pastor abusers on the governing board, it's unlikely that all your church leaders are spiritual rebels. You probably have board members who love the Lord and want to do what's right. Those are the people you need to keep informed when you begin to be attacked. With their support, you can form a united front against the ungodly individuals who thirst for power and loathe pastoral authority.

Unfortunately, many times ungodly people gain seats of authority through manipulating a voting bloc. If your church uses a congregational vote form of government, please consider this option: If the antagonists gained their power through votes, they can also be *voted out* just as easily. Elder-rule churches can do the same.

We believe the case can be made that pastor haters are committing spiritual mutiny against God's leader and have therefore forfeited their right of church membership (Rom. 16:17). If your sympathizers would agree to turn the tables and call for a vote, they could expel the abusers instead of letting them run you off!

It is our hope that your supporters will stand with you. Nevertheless, a distinct possibility exists that, no matter how hard you try to convince others of your integrity, calling, and vision, the silent majority will abandon you and you must face your persecutors alone. As mentioned previously, everyone forsook Paul when he was attacked. Let's continue reading and find out the rest of the story:

> At my first defense no one supported me, but all deserted me; may it not be counted against them. *But the Lord stood with me, and strengthened me* (2 Tim. 4:16-17).

Even though everyone else may have deserted you in this crucial spiritual battle, remember that the Lord is standing with you. In the end, that's all that really matters.

Chapter 7

Do Demons Attend Church?

And they went into Capernaum; and immediately on the Sabbath He entered the synagogue and began to teach . . . And just then there was in their synagogue a man with an unclean spirit; and he cried out, saying, "What do we have to do with You, Jesus of Nazareth? Have You come to destroy us? I know who You are—the Holy One of God!" (Mark 1:21, 23-24)

Don't you find it interesting that a demon was sitting in the synagogue in Capernaum where Jesus preached? What was it doing there? That devil wasn't there to sing praises to God or to learn from Jesus. No doubt this evil spirit had infiltrated the congregation to stir up trouble and create strife. Satan's strategy against God's people has always been to divide and conquer.

If you think this was an isolated incident, just keep reading. "And He went into their *synagogues throughout all Galilee*, preaching and *casting out the demons*" (Mark 1:39). Evidently demons attending synagogues was a widespread problem in that day.

Jesus dealt with the demonic activity by addressing it head on. He didn't sweep it under the rug and pretend it wasn't there. The Lord Jesus cast out the foul spirits and publicly exposed what many of us may not want to admit—demons *do* attend church. These representatives from the dark world infiltrate houses of worship to persecute pastors, divide churches, and fight the work of the Holy Spirit.

In the movie *The Wizard of Oz*, Dorothy and her friends were in the Emerald City, trembling in fear because the magnificent wizard had just scolded them. Just then, Dorothy's little dog Toto scampered over to a booth and pulled back the curtain. Everyone gasped to see a bumbling, nervous man pulling levers and pushing buttons, which created the huge, terrifying image on the screen. Now that his illusion had been exposed, the embarrassed wizard made a frantic attempt to keep them believing the lie. He hurriedly spoke into the microphone, "Pay no attention to that man behind the curtain!"

When it comes to pastor abuse, Satan, the *wizard of wickedness* says, "Pay no attention to that devil behind the curtain!" Although he'd like us to believe he doesn't exist, if we pull back the spiritual veil, we will see Lucifer at the command center. He sics demons on pastors faster than the wicked witch can dispatch flying monkeys on Dorothy.

Paul yanks back the curtain to expose the real enemy when he says, "For our struggle is not against flesh and blood, but against the rulers, against the powers, against the world forces of this darkness, against the spiritual forces of wickedness in the heavenly places" (Eph. 6:12).

What does this have to do with your turbulent situation? More than you might think. The devil is the spiritual force that's causing the chaos in your church. He uses the abusers as his human agents to carry out his fiendish attacks, who might not be aware they are cooperating with Satan.

Contrary to popular belief, demons don't restrict their activities to Africa and other Third World countries. Evil spirits also operate in American churches, and their presence in your services won't be obvious to the naked eye. They don't barge through the church doors with clashing cymbals singing choruses of "Look at me!" Instead, they gain access into the fellowship by cunningly hitchhiking inside with rebellious people, and their attendance can be detected through the turmoil, division, and hatred that surfaces in the flock.

An Example of Remarkable Dedication
Dan has to be one of the most dedicated servants in the church today. Incredibly, he has memorized five entire books of the Bible—word for word. He hopes to have the entire Bible memorized before he dies. By his own admission he spends at least three hours a day in prayer. He's also a faithful giver, contributing substantially more than ten percent of his income to his church.

To ensure he doesn't fall into sin, Dan takes numerous precautions and encourages others to follow his example. He has vowed never to watch a movie, or shop at a convenience store where beer, cigarettes, and pornography are sold. His remarkable commitment and sacrifice puts most American Christians to shame.

What's his secret? "The key is my dedication," Dan explains. "I'm at church every time the doors are open. But where is everyone else? They have time to go to their kids' little league ball games but not for

God. Last week only three of us showed up for the prayer meeting at church. That's a disgrace. Those people who claim to believe in God . . . I don't see them taking a stand against sin like I'm taking. I protested in front of a local bar by myself because everyone else in my church was afraid to join me. They're a bunch of cowards, including the pastor."

Daniel appears to be a perfect role model of boldness and dedication. And that's what is so frightening. You see, Dan isn't a Christian!

Although the other testimonies in this book come from true cases of real people, "Dan" is a fictional person. He's actually your typical Pharisee, who lived two thousand years ago. Members of this Jewish sect memorized the first five books of the Old Testament, prayed three hours a day, and paid tithes on everything from livestock and income down to mint, rue, and herbs (Luke 11:42). And if the 613 Old Testament commands weren't cumbersome enough, they invented even more restrictions called "fence laws" to keep people from straying off the straight and narrow path. They took a strong stand for what they believed and were extremely harsh toward anyone who didn't fall in step with them. The common Jew looked at the Pharisees with the greatest admiration because no one appeared to be more dedicated to their faith than this bunch.

When Jesus began His ministry to reach lost souls, this fanatical sect was ruling the religious world in uncontested glory. As much as the Pharisees allegedly loved the written Word, you would assume they would eagerly embrace the Living Word, as God in the flesh stood before them.

On the contrary. The Pharisees were on the frontline to oppose everything Christ did and taught. These religious leaders, who controlled their synagogues, couldn't recognize Him as the Son of God, even after watching Him perform miracles. "And the blind and the lame came to Him in the temple, and He healed them. But when the chief priests and the scribes saw the wonderful things He had done . . . they became indignant" (Matt. 21:14-15).

When Jesus healed a man's withered hand—right before the very eyes of this scholarly crew, it was as if He had broken every command in the Book. Instead of worshipping at His feet, the Pharisees counseled together "how they might destroy Him" for violating their highly legalistic system (See Mark 3:1-6).

How could these brilliant, dedicated religious leaders, who seemed to be the ideal role models of righteousness, be so misguided? Although they duped the common people into thinking they were the perfect example of holiness, they couldn't fool Jesus. He knew their hearts and repeatedly exposed the Pharisees' hypocrisy throughout the entire span of His ministry.

He aggravated these phonies to no end by refusing to bow down to their insincere piety, or play their silly religious games. Instead of praising them, He rebuked them, calling them a "brood of vipers" and "hypocrites." Then, as if that weren't enough to impose a death sentence upon Himself, He blasted them with another reprimand: "Woe to you, scribes and Pharisees, hypocrites, because you travel about on sea and land to make one proselyte; and when he becomes one, you make him twice as much a son of hell as yourselves" (Matt. 23:15).

Consider who we're talking about. These were the most highly-esteemed religious leaders of the day, who occupied the most coveted positions in their synagogues. It had to stun the listening audience, who had been impressed by the Pharisees, when Jesus publicly denounced them: "Don't be fooled by these hypocrites. God is not like these snakes!"

Imagine how confused the average layperson must have been, in the midst of so many sanctimonious voices claiming ownership of the truth. *All our lives we've been intimidated by the Pharisees' rules and regulations. Should we let them continue to control our synagogues, or follow this new leader who shows us God's love and opens our eyes to the truths of God's Word?*

Stop and think about this, pastor. Could this be the same dilemma your congregation is now facing? Could it be that the church members who are fighting you are actually trying to protect a religious system that they control?

The Spirits Behind Phariseeism

Were the Pharisees controlled by demons? Jesus' scathing rebuke indicated they indeed were. "You are of *your father the devil*, and you want to do *the desires of your father*" (John 8:44). The Lord Jesus pulled back the curtain to expose this truth: the Pharisees listened to and followed Satan's instructions, not God's! These pompous play-actors were actually counterfeit saints, outwardly performing seemingly righteous acts, but inwardly were full of wickedness and corruption.

Their conspiracy to kill the Lord Jesus was in complete cooperation with the most sheer evil genius of all—Satan himself.

Think about it. The devil used men seemingly above reproach, who were revered in the community and displayed all the trappings of godly devotion. The people of that day honored the Pharisees as the most dedicated of all religious leaders. If we lived back then, would we have dared to call into question their relationship with God?

They seemed to show infallible evidence of salvation by memorizing Scriptures, praying, tithing, and fasting. Yet, in God's eyes, they were more evil than the worst of sinners. Jesus told them, "Truly I say to you that the tax-gatherers and harlots will get into the kingdom of God before you" (Matt. 21:31). He looked beyond their public performance and exposed the truth; that their hearts were light-years away from God. "This people honors Me with their lips, but their heart is far away from Me" (Matt. 15:8).

We would not have you ignorant, brethren, so put on your "thinking cap" and ponder this next hard truth. If the Pharisees indeed had demons either indwelling or influencing them, what happened to those wicked "religious" spirits after each of those Pharisees died? Those religious demons are still on earth and have been deceiving people ever since. Could it be they are still utilizing the same strategy as back then? Is it possible that Pharisees are amongst us today, trying to run our churches and run off our pastors—just as they controlled the synagogues and crucified the Lord Jesus?

Evil spirits are fallen angels that have been here on earth since before Adam's fall and won't be cast into the abyss until Judgment Day. They are fully aware of their ever-diminishing time on earth and their ultimate destiny. "And behold, (the demons) cried out, saying, 'What do we have to do with You, Son of God? Have You come here to torment us *before the time*?'" (Matt. 8:29) These wicked spirits pleaded with Jesus not to throw them into the abyss prematurely (see Luke 8:31). That means they are still at work on earth to this day until their appointed time of judgment comes.

Since that's the case, let's try to figure out where they might be right now and what they're up to. You could make an argument that they're inhabiting a herd of pigs somewhere, but it's unlikely. Satan is smarter than to allow his helpers to once again be turned into deviled ham. So if you were the devil, where would you plant your demonic legions, especially the deceitful ones of the religious variety?

It doesn't take an exorcist to figure this one out. They're headed straight for the church buildings, just like they crept into the synagogues. The demonic spirits of Phariseeism are alive today, and are mimicking the same devout behavior in churches as they did in the synagogues two thousand years ago. They'll do everything within their power to infiltrate churches to prevent attendees from experiencing a true relationship with God. Even though the Pharisees became extinct long ago, it's stunning that their devilish script is still being meticulously followed by abusers in today's churches.

Since the devil and his demons can't do anything without cooperation from humans, all they need to do is find someone who lusts for power and loves to glory in religious limelight. They seek for rebellious people—modern-day Pharisees—who crave control and positions of authority, and will carry out every depraved thought and deed planted in their minds. Once the demons and rebels unite, they are energized to fiercely resist any move of God.

We want to be very clear here, lest we be misunderstood. We're not suggesting that you look for a demon in every pew, or that all church members with a differing opinion are demon-possessed. Only God knows whether clergy haters are oppressed, possessed, or merely influenced by fallen angels. Still, who can deny that pastor abusers are *at best* rebellious Christians, who are unwittingly cooperating with the enemy? It's hard for us to understand how these fanatics are not aware that they're being controlled by evil spirits, which fervently seek to destroy thousands of churches.

Again, we're not advocating a witch-hunt. Nevertheless, it's imperative that we recognize the activities taking place in the spiritual realm around us. In an effort to maintain the spirit of unity in the bond of peace, Paul urged us to be on the alert "so that Satan will not outsmart us. For we are very familiar with his evil schemes" (2 Cor. 2:11 NLT).

Not All Demons Act Alike
Demonic activity seems to operate according to a wicked hierarchy of principalities, powers, rulers of the darkness of this world, and spiritual wickedness in high places (Eph. 6:12). From this invisible realm, Satan rules as the "prince of this world" (John 12:31) and the "prince of the power of the air, of the spirit that *is now working in the sons of disobedience*" (Eph. 2:2).

These fallen angels are highly organized, with specific assignments to carry out. For example, a demonic spirit caused a man to be mute:

> And one of the crowd answered Him, "Teacher, I brought You my son, possessed with *a spirit which makes him mute*" . . . And when Jesus saw that a crowd was rapidly gathering, He rebuked the unclean spirit, saying to it, "You *deaf and dumb spirit*, I command you, come out of him and do not enter him again" (Mark 9:17, 25).

Evidently, this demon's task was to make him deaf and dumb, while in another case a spirit made a man blind (see Matt. 12:22). In an even more bizarre account, an evil spirit caused a woman to be bent over double for eighteen years, until Jesus set her free (Luke 13:11-13). Although most physical handicaps have natural explanations, these Scriptures reveal that some illnesses and disorders have been caused by spirits.

Which brings us to our point. These spiritual beings often generate earthly manifestations through planting thoughts and suggestions in unsuspecting minds. While some demons specialize in deafness, dumbness, and blindness, others focus on acting "religious." Once religious demons find cooperative human counterparts, they can easily blend into congregations. Their mission is to imitate Christian lingo and mannerisms so they can build credibility within the fellowship. Of course, the hidden agenda is to persecute the pastor and divide the church.

This cunning strategy to beat up the pastor isn't nearly as obvious in America as it is in other countries. In 2006, five men attended a church service in Turkey. They introduced themselves as newly converted Christians and asked to meet privately with the pastor. No one suspected their real mission until later, when the pastor, Kamil Kiroglu, was discovered bleeding and unconscious on the streets. The men were actually members of Al Qaeda, who had planned to kill him if he didn't deny his Christian faith.

"They were trying to force me to deny Jesus," Kiroglu said. "But each time they asked me to deny Jesus and become a Muslim, I was saying, 'Jesus is Lord.' The more I said 'Jesus is Lord,' the more they beat me." Suddenly, he said, he felt two heavy blows, one on his head and the other on his spine, and everything went dark. When he regained consciousness, his attackers were gone and his friend was trying to wake him up.[44]

Religious Demons Perform Church Duties

The devil cleverly uses widely divergent strategies to deceive and entrap people. While Satan certainly appoints some of his sleazy spirits to tempt people at XXX movie theaters, other devils are delegated to infiltrate church buildings to attack the pastor. These "religious demons" don't act like lewd satanic beings in a porn movie because it would blow their cover. Instead, they specialize in performing church duties, just like they manipulated the Pharisees to act religiously. Some of them even handle church funds, like Judas. But one thing that unites them all is that they deposit evil suggestions in the minds of unruly church members who find fault, complain, and cause division.

The demonic activity usually begins in a small setting. A Sunday school class can turn into a weekly gripe and gossip session. A pastor's wife that we interviewed told her husband, "I'm not going to those women's meetings anymore. You have to backslide to have fellowship with them." The same negativity can take place in a deacon's meeting, or any other discussion group for that matter.

Once a few complainers get enough listeners to agree with them, they'll unleash a deluge of malicious gossip and vicious slander so as to discredit the pastor and spread discord in the church. "Holding to *a form of godliness*, although they have denied its power; and avoid such men as these" (2 Tim. 3:5). Paul exposes the spirit behind them:

> For such men are false apostles, deceitful workers, disguising themselves as apostles of Christ. And no wonder, for even Satan disguises himself as an angel of light. Therefore it is not surprising if *his servants also disguise themselves as servants of righteousness*; whose end shall be according to their deeds. (2 Cor. 11:13-15)

How do these religious demons act in church? They furiously resist every move of God and celebrate when they drive godly shepherds out of the church. A terminated pastor gave this shocking report when he resigned his position:

---

[44] "Pastor Beaten by Five Muslims Claiming Connection to Al Qaeda", February 3, 2006, as quoted in www.persecution.com.

Some unyielding deacons and angry members didn't like my ideas of reaching out to people who don't know Christ, so they forced my resignation. In my final business meeting, I told the congregation, "I believe the Lord is leading me to step down and resign as pastor, effective immediately." As soon as I said that, about fifteen people who had opposed me stood up, started applauding, and shouted, "Hallelujah! Praise God!" In the two years I had been their pastor, they had never clapped in church or shouted praise to God. In fact, they had always opposed displays of emotion in the worship service. I hadn't even seen them smile until I resigned and then they all had big grins on their faces.

False Conversions

If the Pharisees who ruled the synagogues, memorized Scripture, and prayed three hours a day, were headed to hell, why do we assume that someone who is actively involved in church is truly saved? If a Pharisee were to join one of our churches today he would quickly find places to serve, and his incredible dedication would jettison him into a seat of prominence.

Not everyone who wears a fleece is a sheep. The apostle Paul warned, "They profess to know God, but by their deeds they deny Him, being detestable and disobedient, and worthless for any good deed" (Titus 1:16). Let this be a sober reminder that a person can faithfully attend every worship service, teach Sunday school, serve as a deacon, attend prayer meetings, fast, tithe, and even preach—and still not have a personal relationship with Jesus Christ.

Are the abusers who collaborate with the enemy saved or lost? Only God knows for sure. "The Lord knows those who are His," and, "Let everyone who names the name of the Lord abstain from wickedness" (2 Tim. 2:19). The greatest danger in Christendom is serving in church and never being saved in the first place.

Salvation is only by God's grace and is obtained through personal faith in Christ's atoning work on the cross. However, many people attempt to purchase their own salvation through years of faithful service in church, without knowing the Lord Jesus. By far, the most frightening self-deception is a false conversion—to think one is genuinely saved, while actually being desperately lost. Jesus gave this warning to those actively involved in futile religious activities:

> "Not everyone who says to Me, 'Lord, Lord,' will enter the kingdom of heaven; but he who does the will of My Father who is

in heaven. Many will say to Me on that day, 'Lord, Lord, did we not prophesy in Your name, and in Your name cast out demons, and in Your name perform many miracles?' And then I will declare to them, 'I never knew you; depart from Me, you who practice lawlessness.'" (Matt. 7:21-23).

Despite their claims to religious work, these individuals never experienced salvation because Jesus says, "I *never* knew you," and not "I once knew you." Yet, it's staggering that so many fall into this category of deceived people, who were apparently highly involved in church activities. If even a fraction of these unsaved religious people are serving in our churches today, we must assume that some of these people mentioned in Matthew chapter 7 are pastor abusers.

Greater is He who is in You
Perhaps all this talk of spiritual warfare is a bit frightening to you. It shouldn't be, if we clearly understand who we are in Christ. The weakest Christian is more powerful than the strongest demon. God informs us that "Greater is He who is in you than he that is in the world" (1 John 4:4). Jesus gives us authority "over all the power of the enemy, and nothing shall injure you" (Luke 10:19). We don't need to run from Satan in fear because when we resist the devil, the Lord orders him to flee *from us* (James 4:7).

Comparing Satan's power to God's is like contrasting a candle's light to the sun; there is no comparison. When believers come to understand the incredible power and authority we possess as children of God, all fear of the enemy will dissipate. Is the heavyweight boxing champion of the world afraid that a toddler will beat him up? Isn't an atomic bomb more powerful than a BB gun?

The only way the devil can intimidate us is through deception, which is essentially his sole weapon against the believer. He must somehow get us to believe the lie that he's more powerful than Christians. He knows that the only way we'll be afraid of him is if we choose to submit to his lies instead of trusting God's Word.

Pastor, God has called you to stand firm in the armor of the Almighty against the forces of evil (Eph 6:13-18). As you battle the forces that threaten to instigate trouble, don't be afraid because the Lord is with you. Keep ever mindful of His command, "Do not give the devil an opportunity" (Eph. 4:27).

Chapter 8

Submission Is Not a Curse Word

> Obey your leaders, and submit to them; for they keep watch over your souls, as those who will give an account. Let them do this with joy and not with grief, for this would be unprofitable for you. (Heb. 13:17)

From 1918 to 1919, the H1N1 virus, also known as the Spanish flu, killed an estimated 20 million to 100 million people worldwide, including more than 500,000 in the United States.[45] It's astonishing to think that a microscopic virus was so deadly that it sent nearly a hundred million people to their graves prematurely.

I'm sure many observers at that time couldn't figure out why people all over the world were dropping dead for no apparent reason. Logic would tell you that something lethal was at work, even if it wasn't understandable to them. We now know that every one of those fatalities can be traced back to one deadly microbe.

What's driving so many pastors out of churches and ministry? Like the Spanish flu, pastor abuse can be traced back to a single deadly virus called *rebellion*. This little bug, which first germinated under the auspices of Satan in the Garden of Eden, now adds a curse to everything it infects; including the church.

As we take a hard look at the staggering number of pastors calling it quits, we begin to understand that rebellion is the menacing force that's driving them out. Rebellion is a defiant mindset that resents authority, gives the devil access into the fellowship, and unleashes its fury on the most noticeable figure in the church, the pastor. If the assault on God's shepherds isn't stopped, it will expand what has already become an ecclesiastical pandemic.

After Saul had been anointed king over Israel, he turned into a crazed madman, continually hunting down David in an effort to put

---

[45] DeNoon, Daniel J. "Timeline: Avian and Pandemic Influenza" November 2, 2005, Fox News.

him to death. Even though David had opportunities to kill the king, he refused to harm him. His unwavering reverence for God's established authority left him terrified to "touch God's anointed."

Taking the opposite approach of David, many church members today have zero respect for the God-ordained office of pastor, with no fear whatsoever of touching the Lord's anointed. No leader, regardless of how gentle and kind he may be, is exempt from the antagonists' hostility since *submission* isn't in their vocabulary.

Moses, the most humble man on the face of the earth, received heated opposition from Jannes and Jambres (Num. 12:3). The apostle Paul declares that we will encounter the same form of resistance as Moses:

> They will consider nothing sacred. They will be unloving and unforgiving; they will slander others and have no self-control; they will be cruel and have no interest in what is good . . . And these teachers fight the truth just as Jannes and Jambres fought against Moses. Their minds are depraved, and *their faith is counterfeit.*
> (2 Tim. 3:2, 3, 7, 8 NLT)

The Problem: No respect for authority

The late Rodney Dangerfield was best known for his line, "Hey, I get no respect." This sentiment is echoed by pastors, who are persistently maligned by defiant church members. Sometimes the rebels will join together to publicly protest against authority, as one pastor testifies:

> As I was preaching on Sunday morning, one of the rebels got up during the middle of the sermon, angrily stomped out of the church, and slammed the door. Then a few minutes later, another person in that power group walked out and slammed the door.
>
> They planned another protest at our Christmas Eve service. As we sang "Silent Night," I walked down the aisle and lit everyone's candle. When I got to the power group, in a public display of defiance to my leadership, this group of twenty people turned their backs on me so I couldn't light their candles.

It's impossible to please someone with a rebellious heart. E. Stanley Jones once told a story about a little girl who stubbornly refused to mind her mother. No matter what her mother told her to do, the daughter always responded, "I don't want to."

In frustration, the mother finally said, "Okay, then do whatever you want to do."

The girl replied, "I don't want to do what I want to do!"

This attitude of "I don't want to" is characteristic of many who revolt against leadership. We all make a choice between two attitudes toward authority: *respect* it or *resent* it. The choice we make will say a great deal about our relationship with the Lord.

Perhaps it wasn't a coincidence that a basketball sized piece of marble fell from the front overhead entry to the Supreme Court building in Washington, D.C. Although nine sculptural figures line the façade over the entrance, the only chunk of marble that fell came from the figure called "Authority."[46]

Maybe this was a sign from God that He's tired of rebellion against authority, which is nothing more than witchcraft and idolatry. "For rebellion is as the sin of witchcraft, and insubordination is as iniquity and idolatry" (1 Sam. 15:23).

We live in a society that loves to ridicule its leaders. Comedians on late-night shows make fun of the president. Kids badmouth their teachers. Teenagers detest their parents. Employees belittle their bosses. Is it any surprise that some of these anarchists have infiltrated our churches with this attitude?

"I Only Take My Orders from God!"

A minister told us about Pam, who had a long track record of knocking heads with her pastors. Unhappy in her previous church, she joined a new one and began helping with a children's church class. It didn't take long for her to discover that the teaching material the church had authorized wasn't to her liking.

Without seeking permission, Pam single-handedly revamped the program by changing the curriculum and format. Needless to say, this caused immediate confusion with the other teachers who were operating as a team. When the pastor asked why she didn't consult anyone, she defiantly declared, "I only take my orders from the Holy Spirit, not from any person. I won't bow down to anyone!"

Unfortunately, this is a typical response from spiritual rebels. They act in their own self-interest and then claim to be following divine orders. They'll defend their actions by saying, "God told me," which interpreted means, "Who are you to question God?" (One pastor

---

[46] The Beaumont Enterprise, November 29, 2005.

answered the rebellious claim with "God told me that He didn't tell you that!")

They conveniently overlook Scriptures that contradict their insubordinate actions, and ignore the fact that *God has already told them in His Word* to submit to those in authority. When we submit to our church leaders, we *are* submitting to the Lord. Some people never realize that having a respectful attitude toward those in charge is more important to God than running their own agendas.

Rebellion against authority is an act of treason against God. Paul writes:

> Everyone must submit himself to the governing authorities, for there is no authority except that which God has established. The authorities that exist have been established by God. Consequently, he who rebels against the authority is rebelling against what God has instituted, and those who do so will bring judgment on themselves. (Rom. 13:1-3)

The time has come to ask these insurgents, "Which part of this passage do you not understand?" The Bible repeatedly accentuates the importance of submission. Ephesians 4:17-6:9 connects spiritual maturity and submission to authority in marriages, parental relationships and employer-type relationships. Romans 13:1-7, Titus 3:1, and Hebrews 13:17 all exhort believers to submit to civil authorities. First Peter 2:13-14 says, "Submit yourselves for the Lord's sake to every human institution, whether to a king as the one in authority, or to governors as sent by him for the punishment of evildoers and the praise of those who do right."

These texts clearly demonstrate that submission to earthly authorities is a reflection of our willingness to submit to God's ultimate divine authority. However, the reverse is also true. To rebel against the concept of authority is to rebel against the God who created and constituted it.

Yield to the Higher Authority

Are there cases where we should not submit? Yes. If a boss or ruler asks us to do something immoral, unethical, or to disobey God's Word, we are not obligated to submit. When the high priest told Peter and the apostles to stop teaching about Jesus, they responded, "We must obey

God rather than men" (Acts 5:29). Instead of angrily rebelling against the high priest, they chose to humbly submit to the higher authority.

Whenever we encounter situations in which two or more authorities are in conflict, we should yield to the highest one without despising the lower one. I once drove up to an intersection where an accident had occurred. A policeman stood in the intersection directing traffic. Although the traffic light was red, the policeman waved for me to drive through it. Which authority should I obey—the traffic light or the policeman?

In this instance, the traffic cop was a higher authority than the traffic light. And, while I ignored one authority to submit to a higher one here, I didn't rebel against all traffic lights from then on. I respected both, but couldn't obey both at the same time.

If someone cannot agree with the church leadership, he has the freedom to leave the fellowship without causing a ruckus. It's certainly not wrong to change churches, and it's not rebellious to leave a place of worship if the pastoral leadership is morally corrupt or doctrinally unsound. However, once he settles in a new congregation, he must humbly submit himself to the authorities in that place.

Paul understood the importance of respecting our leaders and implored us to pray for them: "I urge you, first of all, to pray for all people. As you make your requests, plead for God's mercy upon them, and give thanks. Pray this way for kings and all others who are in authority, so that we can live in peace and quietness, in godliness and dignity. This is good and pleases God our Savior" (1 Tim. 2:1-3 NLT).

Prayer is precisely what leaders desperately need as the spirit of anarchy seems to be gaining strength by the hour. While intercession not only helps those in charge to make wise decisions, it also keeps our own hearts in check, since it is unlikely we will detest anyone we are praying for.

The Purpose: To maintain order and judge evil.
To ensure that holy people are ruling in His Church, the Lord has set forth biblical qualifications for leadership. Godly leadership, along with submissive followers, are the two dynamics that make an effective church. Hebrews 13:17 (NLT) says, "Obey your spiritual leaders and do what they say. Their work is to watch over your souls, and they know they are accountable to God. Give them reason to do this joyfully and not with sorrow. That would certainly not be for your benefit."

The Corinthian church was in chaos, so Paul reminded them God is not the author of confusion (1 Cor. 14:33). He also added, "But let all things be done properly and in an orderly manner" (1 Cor. 14:40). Just as the planets in our solar system orbit in perfect harmony around the sun, so the Church operates in harmony when it revolves around the Son. Without submission to authority, chaos is guaranteed.

The Lord also established authority for the purpose of judging evil and punishing the evildoer. "For rulers are not a cause of fear for good behavior, but for evil. Do you want to have no fear of authority? Do what is good, and you will have praise from the same; for it is a minister of God to you for good. But if you do what is evil, be afraid; for it does not bear the sword for nothing; for it is a minister of God, an avenger who brings wrath upon the one who practices evil" (Rom. 13:3, 4).

It's imperative that all leaders in the church meet scriptural qualifications and are godly individuals who are morally above reproach. If biblical standards are ignored, pastor abusers will grab seats of authority, and will persecute the righteous instead of punishing the wicked. "When the righteous are in authority, the people rejoice; but when a wicked man rules, the people groan" (Prov. 29:2 NKJV).

The Principle: Submission works voluntarily from the bottom up.
It's nearly impossible to find a church where everyone is in agreement on every issue. To keep ministry flowing smoothly, its members must overrule their own preferences through submission, so that the greater good can be accomplished.

The Greek word for submission means "to yield under authority." It is an attitude of the heart that joyfully volunteers to respect those in authority over them. Paul writes, "But we request of you, brethren, that you appreciate those who diligently labor among you, and have charge over you in the Lord and give you instruction, and that you esteem them very highly in love because of their work. Live in peace with one another" (1 Thess. 5:12-13). Think how much good churches could accomplish if every member had this attitude!

There's only one hitch. A pastor cannot make anyone submit. This spiritual attitude has to be *their* idea, not yours. It's initiated internally, not externally, and works from the bottom of the hierarchy up, not from the top down. When this godly way of thinking is birthed inside a person's spirit, submitting becomes as natural as breathing. The entire kingdom of God is set up to operate through yielding to His chosen leaders.

Dictators, on the other hand, wield their authority with brute force in an attempt to coerce people into compliance. That only creates intimidation, not submission. And that's why a dictatorial leadership in a church never works. It creates an adversarial relationship between the pastor and the congregation, which fosters anger and strife.

On the other hand, biblical submission willfully yields the right-of-way to those divinely appointed. Pastors should create such a warm atmosphere in the church that it makes the flock *want* to follow. It's this kind of loving relationship that allows the church to harmoniously function and flourish.

The Promise: Submissive people receive authority from God.
Whenever we surrender ourselves to something, we place ourselves under its power. We are, in effect, choosing to let it control us. If we yield to temptation, it controls us. If we yield to the Holy Spirit, He controls us.

In God's kingdom, the Lord promotes people to leadership who have a track record of humbly submitting themselves. Submission is the pathway to receiving authority. This is why James tells us: "Submit therefore to God. Resist the devil and he will flee from you" (James 4:7). Submission to the Lord gives us the authority to resist the devil.

A Roman centurion officer asked Jesus to heal his slave. Jesus said, "I will come and heal him." The centurion answered, "Lord, I am not worthy for You to come under my roof, but just say the word, and my servant will be healed" (Matt. 8:7-8).

He didn't try to manipulate Jesus by bragging, "I am a man *in* authority." Instead he humbly said, "I too am a man *under* authority." The centurion could order his soldiers to come and go because he received his authority by submitting to the officers above him. The soldiers beneath him obeyed because they understood the Roman chain of command. The centurion's orders carried the same authority as if they came from the Emperor himself.

When the centurion said, "I too am a man under authority," he understood that Jesus had also submitted Himself. Because the Son was submitted to the Father, Christ's words carried the Father's authority. Jesus could order the slave's infirmity to leave and it would have to obey—just like the soldiers had to leave when the centurion ordered them to go. The Roman centurion understood an important principal: authentic authority is acquired through obediently submitting.

Jesus marveled at this centurion's faith. The Greek word *marveled* means "astonished." He was astonished to find someone who understood the reciprocal relationship between authority and submission. Our Lord probably marvels today whenever He sees someone cheerfully submitting to authority.

Christ turned to His followers and said, "Do you see this Gentile? I want you to learn from him. He has more faith than anyone in Israel because he understands how submission and authority work."

In contrast, spiritual rebels will attempt to seize authority through manipulation and intimidation, which disqualifies them from leadership. Jesus said, "The scribes and the Pharisees have *seated themselves* in the chair of Moses" (Matt. 23:2).

Just as the Pharisees illegitimately elevated themselves to places of authority, pastor abusers will also grab seats of power using illicit methods. After the insurgents capture the control panel, they will wage war with anyone who comes near it. For this reason, if a pastor accepts a call to that church, he'll have to fight unending battles with the rebels already in charge.

The Penalty: Remove those who instigate turmoil and division.
Submission is a curse word for rebellious people and that's why Paul instructs the church leaders to "admonish the unruly" (1 Thess. 5:14). Insubordinate church members must be treated differently than those who joyfully cooperate to build God's kingdom.

Confronting those who disrupt the church can be a daunting task for those who oversee the flock. If church leaders acquiesce to their intimidation, it signals weakness, which gives them permission to continue in their anarchy. Peter writes these words of assurance to the fainthearted: "And do not fear their intimidation, and do not be troubled" (1 Pet. 3:14).

Suppose you're watching a basketball game, when you notice a particular player tripping and elbowing other players. He's causing chaos on the court and you're wondering how he's getting away with it. The referee is supposed to penalize the disruptive players but nothing's happening. By now he should have received five fouls and been ejected from the game.

As the game proceeds, you notice the unruly player hit his opponent in the back of the head. Not wanting to cause a disturbance, the referee whispers to the offender, "Was that an accident or did you hit him on purpose?"

The athlete answers, "Oh, it was just an accident."

"No problem, I understand," says the ref, and the game continues.

One minute later, the troublemaker pushes another player down. The ref inquires again, "Was that your fault or his?"

The obstinate player says, "Hey, don't blame me. He got in my way." The referee sheepishly walks away.

Next, this rowdy renegade sticks out his foot and trips a member of the other team. This time, the referee finally blows his whistle and stops play.

"How many times have I told you to play nicely?" he asks, exasperated. "I'm about to run out of patience with you. The next time you do something like that, you'll be sorry!"

Soon, another infraction occurs. "Why did you do that?" the referee pleads.

The player replies with a smirk, "Because I felt like it! And I'm not sorry either. So what are you going to do about it?"

Holding his head in his hands, the referee thinks, *I'm not sure how to handle this guy.* The official allows him to keep playing without reprimand.

As the clock ticks on, his fouls become more frequent and blatant. He's deliberately pushing, tripping, and hitting everyone. But the referee never gives him a penalty or kicks him out of the game.[47]

Just as a basketball game has rules for its players, so does the church. Contentious and disruptive members shouldn't be allowed to remain in the game any longer than an out-of-control basketball player.

Unfortunately, many pastors are like the ref in the story—afraid to confront those unruly individuals who create friction in the church. Nevertheless, the Scriptures are unmistakable; if someone continues to cause turmoil and strife, he must be confronted. It isn't easy, and demands courage to stand up to troublemakers, but for the sake of the common good, it must be done. (See the story about Divisive Dave in chapter five).

Pastor, you are the referee, and if they continue to foul they must be ejected. However, before you go on a witch-hunt, make sure you correctly identify the virus. Rebels are not those members who won't

---

[47] Rosemond, John K. *Six Point Plan for Raising Happy, Healthy Children*, Andrews McNeel Publishing, 53-55.

volunteer because they're too busy, too tired, or too lazy. Sure, they don't contribute much, but for the most part they're harmless. These aren't the ones to worry about. It's the rabble-rousers that continually create friction and division who must be warned, and possibly even ejected from the church.

Four Reasons for Church Discipline

Scripture speaks of four situations that require expulsion from the congregation:

- **Rebellious people who create strife and division in the church:** "Reject a factious man after a first and second warning" (Titus 3:10).
- **Unrepentant Christians who openly flaunt sexual immorality in the church:** "For what have I to do with judging outsiders? Do you not judge those who are within the church? But those who are outside, God judges. Remove the wicked man from among yourselves" (1 Cor. 5:12-13).
- **False teachers who cause division:** "Now I beseech you, brethren, mark them which cause divisions and offences contrary to the doctrine which ye have learned; and avoid them" (Rom. 16:17).
- **A Christian who is unrepentant of a particular sin:** "And if your brother sins, go and reprove him in private; if he listens to you, you have won your brother. But if he does not listen to you, take one or two more with you, so that by the mouth of two or three witnesses every fact may be confirmed. And if he refuses to listen to them, tell it to the church; and if he refuses to listen even to the church, let him be to you as a Gentile and a tax-gatherer" (Matt. 18:15-17).

Matthew 18 is wrongly understood in most churches as the sole procedure for church discipline. By applying this Scripture inappropriately, the church completely ignores the correct procedure for rebellion, mentioned in Titus 3:10. Ken Newberger wisely observes:

> I reviewed some 40 church bylaws. Not surprisingly, virtually every one of them had a section on church discipline, (but) not one had a section on how that church would deal with the disagreements and disputes that

regularly appear in congregational life apart from Matthew 18. This poses a very real problem.

Because of a lack of alternatives, churches try to squeeze all dispute resolution into the Matthew 18 model of church discipline (which only) applies when unrepentant sin is involved. Matthew 18 applies when there are at least two or three witnesses of the sin. When witnesses to the sin do not exist, the process cannot move forward.[48]

Too often, Matthew 18 is interpreted to mean that the witnesses are to observe the conversation between the parties, as if that itself will uncover truth. If Pete charges Beth with sin and Beth denies it, what good are witnesses to the conversation? If such a charge made in front of observers is allowed to stand, where is the protection against false accusation?[49]

It's for this reason God gave us different instructions for those who create strife. The one who causes division should be expelled after only *two* warnings (Titus 3:10). Divisive people are usually aggressive and hostile, and must be dealt with swiftly. This two-step strategy must be utilized to remove the pastor abusers from the congregation.

The first admonition should be an explanation of their wrongdoing and a demand that it cease. The second warning is a final notice that no further disruptive behavior will be tolerated, or excommunication will be imminent. Nowhere in Scripture does it say that the troublemakers must be brought before the whole church. This important matter must be handled by the elders and senior pastor, without involving the congregation.

Furthermore, no other instructions are given for exactly how to carry it out. It just says to purge the antagonist from the church. The simplest way might be for the senior pastor and leadership team to visit the rebel's house and inform him that he has been removed from church membership due to insubordination—and that the decision is final.

How should the congregation be informed that the person has been expelled? Allow the Holy Spirit to lead you. In some cases, no

---

[48] Jesus quoted from Deut. 19:15: "Only on the evidence of two witnesses or of three witnesses shall a charge be established." Num. 35:30 says, "No person shall be put to death on the testimony of one witness." This is why Paul writes, "Do not admit a charge against an elder except on the evidence of two or three witnesses" (1 Tim. 5:19).

[49] Newberger, Ken. "When Church Discipline is Appropriate and When It Is Not" www.resolvechurchconflict.com.

announcement needs to be made. In larger churches, most people wouldn't even know the individual, so no explanation is required. In smaller churches where everyone is familiar the person, you may need to give a short statement that the troublemaker had to be removed according to the command of Titus 3:10.

It might be best to make a public announcement in a specially-called meeting, or through a letter sent to the congregation. Explain that the action had to be taken to keep peace in the church, the decision is final, and it's time to move forward.

However, restoration of a person who fell into a particular sin is a completely different matter with different instructions. Paul wrote: "Dear brothers and sisters, if another Christian is overcome by some sin, you who are godly should gently and humbly help that person back onto the right path" (Gal. 6:1 NLT). In contrast to removing an antagonist who is disrupting the church, confronting fallen Christians becomes a *three*-step process, with each action intent upon repentance and restoration.

Initially, go privately to the individual. If that fails, step two is to take with you one or two people who have witnessed the offense. Finally, as a last resort (step number three) bring the matter before the church.

Apparently this process involves a backslidden person who is still actively attending church. He wants to be involved with the church but also wants to live an immoral lifestyle. The purpose of step three is to force the person decide which is more important to him, the Lord or the world. If he repents, he chooses the Lord.

After the matter is discussed and he still won't repent, "let him be to you as a Gentile and a tax-gatherer" (Matt. 18:17). In other words, he is ex-communicated and is no longer a part of that congregation. That sounds unloving until we remember Jesus Christ Himself instructed us to do this.

If a backslidden person has already chosen to leave the fellowship, he has in effect removed himself, which would make the third step of bringing it before the congregation unnecessary. The first two steps were attempts to bring him back into fellowship, but in the end he chose the world instead.

The Purpose of Church Discipline
The purpose of church discipline is to protect the church from people who are trying to destroy it. False teachers must be removed to

maintain sound Biblical doctrine (see 2 Tim. 4:3-4). Unrepentant members must be removed to safeguard the purity of the fellowship (see 1 Cor. 5:6-7). And pastor abusers must be removed to preserve the congregation's peace and unity.

The right to exercise church discipline needs to be included in the bylaws of the church. If the two-step process isn't clearly spelled out, pastor abusers won't be deterred from their insidious plots to attack God's shepherds.

Chapter 9

Closing the Loophole

> When the righteous are in authority, the people rejoice; but when a wicked man rules, the people groan. (Prov. 29:2 NKJV)

You're on your way to the store, when suddenly, you can hardly believe your eyes. You blink, shake your head, then look again. Sure enough, it's a confused dog, trying to walk backwards down the street! Its tail is blindly leading the body, with its head being dragged behind. Just when you thought you'd seen it all, the mutt stops, and does something even more unusual. The tail starts wagging the dog! You think, *That pooch's tail wants to be the head. Doesn't it know he could easily move forward if he'd just turn around?*

Although we snicker at this bizarre anecdote, if we are honest with the facts, we'll have to admit this is exactly how many churches function. The tail wags the dog. Ungodly laity, who should be following their shepherds, have seized control and are leading. Godly shepherds, who should be leading, are reluctantly following the abusers' orders or they'll be terminated. The followers lead and the leaders follow, as the tail wags the dog. It's all backwards and not the way God intends for His church to be led.

It's not normal for sheep to lead shepherds, whether it's on the farm or in the fellowship. Yet in many churches we find the roles reversed, which creates enormous problems for pastors when they try to lead the flock.

The Pastor Abuse Loophole
The root of the pastor abuse problem comes from unqualified, ungodly people occupying positions of authority who are driven by the spirit of rebellion. How do these antagonists get into power in the first place? Somewhere along the way, they took advantage of a loophole in church government and were voted up the chain of command into the seats they occupy.

Many Baptist pastors indicate that some deacons, who give them the most trouble, were not scrutinized closely enough before being elected. In many cases, they're already entrenched in power before the pastor arrives on the scene. The same can be said about lay leaders in other denominations as well. They've been voted into power through a lackadaisical review process that winks at candidates' flaws. If we're ever going to solve the pastor abuser problem, this gigantic loophole needs to be closed.

One pastor shared the following account, which demonstrates why candidates for church offices should be carefully screened before being nominated.

> Not long after I became their pastor, I was in a meeting with our deacons where we discussing nominations for new deacons. In the past, a list was distributed of every man's name in the membership registry as a potential candidate. But I wanted them to consider qualifications instead of popularity.
>
> I said, "Our staff and others in this room know confidential information about some well-known members that would immediately disqualify them. If the congregation nominates an unqualified candidate, we would have to prohibit him from serving. Then everyone in the church would want to know why we rejected him, and it would unnecessarily embarrass the candidate. Before we allow the congregation to vote, let's come up with the names of men that you think would fit the scriptural guidelines for this position."
>
> Six men were suggested and their names were written on a blackboard. I pointed to the first name and asked, "Does anyone know why this man wouldn't qualify?"
>
> One man raised his hand and pointed out a major concern. Several others agreed, so his name was erased from the board. Another candidate had been privately going through serious counseling. The third person was experiencing marriage problems and was on the brink of a divorce. At the end of the discussion, all six names were erased from the blackboard because all had major issues that weren't publicly known.
>
> "Do you see the point?" I asked. "If we hadn't gone through this exercise, these men probably would have been elected by the congregation and we would have unqualified men serving as deacons."
>
> My instructional lesson went over like a lead balloon. It never dawned on me that the deacons who were listening to me in that room also had major problems in their personal lives which should have

disqualified them! They got together less than a year later and forced me to resign.

Does Voting Determine God's Will?

A pastor of a large congregation in Georgia believed God was calling him to be the shepherd of a church in another city. He told us, "The new congregation unanimously voted to call me as their pastor. At the same time, my existing flock didn't want me to leave, so they unanimously voted to keep me."

How could both congregations claim that the Lord was guiding them in their decisions and yet reach opposite conclusions? God doesn't contradict Himself, "for He cannot deny Himself" (2 Tim. 2:13). Obviously, one of the churches had to be *totally* wrong, unless you use the wisdom of Solomon and split the baby down the middle. In spite of their unanimous vote, an entire congregation wanted their will to be done instead of what God desired!

It stops to make you wonder how much is going on in our churches today that's actually being initiated by the Lord. We might be shocked if we found out. If a whole congregation missed God's will when they voted incorrectly on their pastor, can you see how easy it would be to elect pastor abusers into power?

The majority is often wrong when it comes to decision-making. The Pharisees, who hated Jesus, stirred up the crowd so Barabbas would receive the vote to be released. Most of Israel ignored Samuel's wise counsel and chose Saul to be their king. The centurion on the prison ship ignored Paul's warning and listened to the majority vote instead.

> [Paul] said to them, "Men, I perceive that the voyage will certainly be attended with damage and great loss, not only of the cargo and the ship, but also of our lives." But the centurion was more persuaded by the pilot and the captain of the ship, than by what was being said by Paul. And because the harbor was not suitable for wintering, *the majority reached a decision* to put out to sea from there... (Acts 27:10-12).

How do pastor abusers get voted into power? In some churches, they're elected simply because they've been members of the church for a long time. Those who vote for them wrongly assume that their longevity somehow qualifies them to lead the church. In other cases, they're elected to authoritative positions simply because no one else wants the responsibility.

It's appalling that so many churches completely ignore the scriptural standards for these esteemed offices. Although the candidates may have serious character flaws which should disqualify them from leadership, the red flags are ignored and the troublemakers are granted ecclesiastical seats.

Why aren't they examined more closely? Because it's far easier to promote the nominee than it is to tell him he's been rejected because he's not qualified. Who has the courage to inform Harry Hothead, a wealthy and well-known businessman, that he doesn't meet the scriptural requirements to serve on the board? When was the last time you heard of a church member being turned down from being an elder or deacon because he was a malicious gossiper, couldn't get along with others, or had a dysfunctional personality?

In all probability, you've never heard of a layperson being screened that closely. This lack of scrutiny is the loophole that pastor abusers use to get into seats of power.

Closing the Loophole
When the unconsecrated, the backslidden, the unsaved, the ungodly, the under-aged, and the newly saved are allowed to cast ballots on important decisions, bedlam is sure to follow. How would these people understand enough about the will of God to make correct judgments? Pastor abusers understand that these people can be easily manipulated and persuaded.

Imagine Moses saying to the Israelites, "Folks, could we have a show of hands for all those of you who would like to continue on into Canaan?" If he would have let the discontented Hebrews to organize a campaign and take a vote, they would have immediately returned to Egyptian bondage.

Many times the Lord's paths are the most difficult ones to travel on, which makes them unpopular with those who are only seeking comfort and status quo. In these cases, a groundswell of complainers in the congregation may drown out the voice of God's shepherds, which again makes the tail wag the dog.

Instead of allowing everyone to have a voice and a vote in running the church, a better option is to have spiritually mature laypersons and pastors at the helm who will seek the will of God in every matter. This group may be called by different names in your church; elders, deacons, bishops, the session, the council, presbytery, leadership team, trustees, church staff, the board, or some other name. Whatever designation your church uses isn't nearly as important as the spiritual health and integrity of the board members.

This ruling group should consist of responsible, kind-hearted believers, whose lives exhibit the fruit of the Spirit. The church should conduct a thorough background check before calling a pastor to ensure the candidate is biblically qualified and a person of integrity. In the same way, laymen who desire offices of church authority should also be held to the identical moral and spiritual standards. When the leadership team possesses these honorable qualities, it's highly likely they will make wise decisions, and it also closes the loophole for pastor abuse.

Qualifications for Spiritual Leaders
The apostle Paul never mentioned anything in his letters about the order of business meetings or voting. Instead, he placed the utmost priority on the moral character and spiritual maturity of the candidates who are considered for positions in the church. Anyone not meeting the criteria should be eliminated from consideration. In case you haven't figured it out yet, the qualifications mentioned in Scripture are designed to keep certain individuals *out* of office.

As we read through the restrictive list, the number of people who fit the job description becomes less and less. God purposely provided this checklist to narrow down the candidates—and to ensure that abusers don't get into power.

Because the readers of this book represent various forms of church government with different titles for its leaders other than "elder," we suggest that you substitute your own denominational title for the office of spiritual leader. We also know that many churches have women faithfully serving in various ministries. We use the word "he" throughout the book because most pastors are male, but that doesn't mean women are not also fulfilling valuable roles in God's kingdom. The requirements for integrity apply to all ministry leaders and servants in His Church.

The purpose of this book is not to debate the correct form of church government and other related issues, but to agree on the common denominator that makes churches function properly—certifying that leaders meet the qualifications.

An elder (anyone in church leadership) is to be above reproach, the husband of one wife, temperate, prudent, respectable, and hospitable

(Titus 1:6, 1 Tim 3:1-2). He should be chosen on the merits of how well he rules his own family: "He must be one who manages his own household well, keeping his children under control with all dignity, but if a man does not know how to manage his own household, how will he take care of the church of God?"(1 Tim. 3:4-5).

Why would Paul require that church leaders manage their families well if it didn't apply to ruling in the church? A father with rebellious children will most likely raise a church family of rebels. If he won't discipline his own kids, how could he be courageous enough to exercise church discipline against an in-your-face church member? Moreover, a father who asks his children's permission every time he makes a decision will have a dysfunctional family with self-centered children. It's the proverbial tail wagging the dog again.

Typically, they were older, mature Christians, hence the term "elders." Because of their knowledge of the Scriptures and wisdom gained from life's experiences, they were the counselors who guided the church by example and advice. Elders couldn't be new converts because they weren't mature enough to make wise spiritual decisions for the congregation (1 Tim. 3:6). Pride is a malady for us all, and could easily sway a new Christian in the wrong direction in the decision-making process.

Elders are called by God to rule in the affairs and ministries of the church (1 Tim. 3:1; 5:17; Titus 1:5). Because they must be "above reproach," they are disqualified if they have a moral or ethical failure (1 Tim. 3:2, 5:7, Titus 1:6-7). These leaders must be free from the love of money, which will keep them from stealing offerings or misappropriating funds.

Additionally, this office requires the leader to be free from addictions and not contentious (1 Tim. 3:3). They must be "able to teach" indicating that they are knowledgeable in the Scriptures (1 Tim. 3:2, 2 Tim. 2:2, 24), although this doesn't mean they must take turns preaching. Shepherds are not to act like tyrants or dictators, but prove themselves to be examples to the flock (1 Pet. 5:3).

In addition, they refute those who contradict sound teaching and fight off wolves when they attack (Titus 1:9, Acts 20:28-29). Paul warned the elders about the wolves (they love lamb chops) that would enter the church and become influential enough to lead people away. It takes guts for an elder to protect the flock.

The pastor should be the head elder, as a first among equals, working in conjunction with the other leaders. If any leader, including the pastor, gets out of line, the brethren will hold that person accountable. In this way, the leaders are monitored by trusted, mature believers, and not by manipulative, rebellious people following their own agenda. This seals off the loophole that pastor abusers use to attack the shepherd.

Qualifications for Servants

The Greek word "deacon" is *diakonos*, which literally means a "humble servant."[50] Deacon is rendered an attendant, helper, and errand runner, which means this person is called to help, support, and encourage pastors. Jesus is the role model for deacons: "Just as the Son of Man did not come to be served, but to serve, and to give His life a ransom for many" (Matt. 20:28).

Deacons must have dignity (respectable, not slanderers), not double-tongued (not hypocritical; saying one thing to one person and something else to another), beyond reproach (Christ-like and without blame), the husband of one wife, and good managers of their children (1 Tim. 3:8-13). Women must be dignified, not malicious gossips, temperate, and faithful in all things (1 Tim. 3:11).

Elders are assigned as the church's rulers and decision-makers.[51] "Let the elders who *rule* well be considered worthy of double honor, especially those who work hard at preaching and teaching" (1 Tim. 5:17). Deacons, on the other hand, are not appointed to be rulers or leaders, but servants. The role of deacons is to carry out, under the elders' oversight, the lesser tasks of the church so that the elders can give their attention to more important things.[52] The distinction is clear; elders are to rule and provide leadership, and deacons are to humbly serve under them (1 Tim. 3:4-5, 10).

In most Baptist churches the pastor is considered the elder of the congregation. Sadly, in many cases that we've heard, some deacons have forsaken their role as servants and have usurped the pastor's authority. Every Baptist pastor that we interviewed told us that their fiercest abusers have been deacons. These counterfeit servants have corrupted the office of deacon—despising pastoral authority, misusing their position, and forcing shepherds out of their churches.

---

[50] *The Bible Knowledge Commentary on the New Testament,* Walvoord & Zuck, Editors, Wheaton, IL: Victor Books, 1983, 737.
[51] See Acts 15:2-6, 22.
[52] *The Bible Knowledge Commentary on the New Testament,* 737.

Nowhere in Scripture do we find deacons fighting their pastors and firing them! Yet in today's church, this is as common as baked beans at a church potluck. Something is terribly wrong here.

Certainly not all deacons are rebellious toward their pastors, and many are godly individuals who love the Lord. But it cannot be denied that ungodly deacons are responsible for driving multitudes of pastors out of their churches through forced termination. We cannot ignore this very clear strategy of the enemy to pervert the office of deacon for the purpose of persecuting pastors.

Keeping the Godly in Charge

After lay leaders have met scriptural requirements, how is the best way to ensure that godly individuals will continue to rule the church? It seems obvious that the current godly leaders would be most qualified to choose future leaders from among the men they are mentoring. Paul wrote: "And the things that you have heard from me among many witnesses, commit these to faithful men who will be able to teach others also" (2 Tim. 2:2 NKJV). This Scripture specifies that future leaders must also be qualified according to their faithfulness. Younger, godly disciples will eventually replace the older elders, which will ensure future stability in church leadership.

Ideally, it would be best for the existing godly leaders to hand-pick the new leaders, making sure they are qualified, and then allow the congregation to confirm their decision. After the candidate is vetted by the existing leaders, the nominee could be presented to the congregation by saying, "If you know of any reason why this person would be disqualified from serving, you must let the board know within two weeks." This allows the congregation to bring to light anything the candidate might be hiding, and the elders can reverse their decision if the new information disqualifies the person.

The apostles Paul and Barnabas prayerfully selected and appointed their leaders after seeking God's wisdom through prayer and fasting: "And when they had *appointed elders* for them in every church, having prayed with fasting, they commended them to the Lord in whom they had believed (Acts 14:23). Paul wrote Titus: "For this reason I left you in Crete, that you might set in order what remains, and *appoint elders* in every city as I directed you" (Titus 1:5).

Why would Timothy and Titus need to appoint elders in these churches if the congregations were voting in their own leaders? One reason might be because the laity were carnal or immature believers and thus unqualified to discern God's will, which is also true in many churches today.

Obviously, someone needed to choose the leaders, and Paul decided to place that responsibility in the hands of the existing godly leadership. However, your church bylaws may specify a different process for electing leaders, and you will need to follow those guidelines, keeping in mind that anyone selected for office needs to be qualified.

The church leadership issue can be confusing with our present-day terminology. Large congregations are usually overseen by their numerous staff personnel; senior pastor, executive pastor, youth pastor, children's pastor, small group pastor, and many other titles. Every minister should be scrutinized for integrity, competence, and giftedness. While some staff pastors may function in the office of elder, others may not. For the church to operate in harmony, all staff members must receive their designated authority from the elders and work in conjunction with them.

Although staff personnel may be spiritually gifted for ministry, they aren't necessarily qualified to be elders. For instance, a youth pastor might enjoy a fruitful ministry with young people but may lack the maturity to be an elder. No matter what the staff position may be, spiritual maturity and godly integrity are essential to serve in this capacity.

Choosing Leaders

Choosing quality leaders isn't rocket science. In every church, people fall under three categories: those who *help*, those who *hide*, and those who *hinder*. It's incumbent upon the leadership team to consider the ministry history of all candidates for church positions before they are appointed.

Would the church gossip make a fitting choice for leading the counseling ministry? Should a dishonest person who doesn't tithe be the church treasurer? Can a divisive person ever unite and strengthen a church? You might be surprised at how many of these personalities have been chosen simply because someone blindly pushed them forward.

We would be wise to remember this profound truth: "He who is faithful in a very little thing is faithful also in much; and he who is unrighteous in a very little thing is unrighteous also in much" (Luke 16:10). Why would God give dynamite to someone who can't handle a firecracker? You get the idea. Don't ignore a person's track record because it reveals his past performance—which is an excellent indicator of what he's planning to do.

A biblically called and qualified leadership team will demonstrate these characteristics:

1) Leaders need a heart for God. Jesus gave us the greatest commandment when He said, "'You shall love the Lord your God with all your heart, and with all your soul, and with all your mind.' This is the great and foremost commandment. The second is like it, 'You shall love your neighbor as yourself'" (Matt. 22:37-39). We must fulfill the Great Commandment before we can carry out the Great Commission. Make sure the candidate loves the Lord and is above reproach in integrity. Someone with a polluted heart will be a bad leader and will likely contaminate others.

2) Leaders need a unified vision. The candidate should want the church to move in the same direction that God is showing His leaders. Unity of vision brings stability to a church, but division is caused by two visions leading in different directions. Paul told the confused Corinthians, "Become complete. Be of good comfort, be of one mind, live in peace; and the God of love and peace will be with you" (2 Cor. 13:11 NKJV).

3) Leaders need a strong backbone. Being a leader isn't for the timid or weak. Complainers usually try to get their way by pulling on the ear of the weakest leader. If you allow a spineless candidate to be elected, he may well become the new spokesperson for the discontented group. It takes courage to oppose antagonists, and the Lord will stand with you. God says, "Have I not commanded you? Be strong and courageous! Do not tremble or be dismayed, for the Lord your God is with you wherever you go" (Josh. 1:9).

If any one of these three traits is lacking, this person will be more of a hindrance than a help. Remember, a small crack in the dam now will result in a flood of irreparable damage later.

We would be amiss if we didn't mention leaders who have "family ties" with pastor abusers. Be extremely wary about choosing a leader who is related to an antagonist. In our interview with abused pastors, we have found that troublemakers are often connected though bloodlines. Family members have been known to "gang up" against the pastor, and if they have one of their own in leadership, it works to their favor.

Even when a member appears to be supportive of you, if he has a relative who is determined to bring you down, the abuser will seize the opportunity. Your antagonist will exploit this family relationship and will apply pressure on the relative to hand over power in some way.

You're probably familiar with Tobiah, who continually opposed Nehemiah when he was rebuilding the wall of Jerusalem (See Neh. 2:10, 19, 4:7-8). Tobiah was related to Eliashib the priest, who held an important position in the temple. Tobiah took advantage of this blood relationship and persuaded Eliashib to prepare a room for him in the house of God. Unbelievably, the priest permitted Nehemiah's chief opponent to reside in the temple complex! This shows how pastor abusers will manipulate relatives who are in power and use them to gain access to key positions in the church.

Nehemiah went ballistic when he found out about "the evil that Eliashib had done for Tobiah by preparing a room for him in the courts of the house of God" (Neh. 13:7). He was so angry that he went to the temple and tossed out all of Tobiah's household goods and cleansed the room of its defilement (13:8-9). He also drove out another relative of both Eliashib and Sanballat, who was another enemy of Nehemiah (13:27). Pastors would be wise to follow Nehemiah's example and quickly remove those who give favoritism to the family tree instead of listening to the Holy Spirit.

No matter which governing model your church utilizes, if you have leaders that meet the three qualifications listed above, God can bless the decision-making process. "But we request of you, brethren, that you appreciate those who diligently labor among you, and have charge over you in the Lord and give you instruction, and that you esteem them very highly in love because of their work. Live in peace with one another" (1 Thess. 5:12-13).

Defining the Lines of Responsibility
All responsibility is delegated from authority, and those receiving it must be held accountable to insure its completion. In ancient Rome, whenever an arch was being constructed, the engineer assumed accountability for his work in the most profound way—by standing under the arch as the capstone was hoisted into place.

In a similar way, church leaders must stand accountable for their decisions. That requires that areas of responsibility need to be clearly defined. Dr. Ken Newberger gives this wise advice:

An essential need within the church is to explicitly establish an infrastructure with well-defined lines of authority. Clearly delineating where individual boundaries of authority begin and end and where overlapping boundaries of authority begin and end is foundational for creating a church environment of stability.

The roles of senior pastor, staff, elders, deacons, trustees, etc. need to be clearly defined. A practical way to better define roles and relationships is to use the "concentric circle approach." Let the pastor start with what he considers to be his smallest circle, elders, for example. Determine where their respective boundaries end and overlap. Ask hypothetical, "what if" scenario questions. Discuss and determine what is required to officially make a decision (e.g. a majority, a supermajority, unanimity).

After each group has gone through this process, widen the circle. Consider the relationship between the elders and the deacons. Where do their respective boundaries end or overlap? How should an impasse between these two groups be addressed? Again ask the hypothetical, "what if" questions.[53]

Following those guidelines may help you resolve the conflict in your congregation. Although you're probably discouraged if abusers are currently controlling your church government, that doesn't mean you should resign as pastor. God can still use you, even in a less-than-ideal situation. You can do some things to improve your situation, which is discussed in the next chapter.

---

[53] Newberger, Ken. "Who's the Boss at Church When Everyone Wants Control?" www.resolvechurchconflict.com, November 4, 2004.

Chapter 10

21 Things You Can Do Right Now

But if any of you lacks wisdom, let him ask of God, who gives to all men generously and without reproach, and it will be given to him. (James 1:5)

When John Huss was arrested and informed that he would be burned to death for his faith, he purposely practiced holding his hand over fire to get ready for his final test. He burned himself in preparation so he could to be faithful to the end.[54]

Though we wish it were different, the words *ministry* and *attack* need to be mentioned together more often by seminary professors. If they were, pastoral graduates would know that preparing for battering is just as necessary as preparing for sermons.

If you've been caught off-guard by the barrage of assaults, don't be immobilized by the paralysis of analysis. The worst thing you can do when you're under attack is to curl up in a fetal position and suck your thumb. Get up and do something! Listed below are twenty-one action points to help bring peace, hope, and stability into your situation

1. Put your complete trust in the Lord.
What you trust is where you put your confidence. Ask yourself, *Am I trusting the provision or the Provider?* A church paycheck is not your source of livelihood. Only God is. "How blessed is the man who has made the Lord his trust, and has not turned to the proud, nor to those who lapse into falsehood" (Ps. 40:4).

You may think you're facing the most frightening financial drought of your entire life. And you fear the world is about to end as you have experienced it thus far. Not really. God has been watching over you and He's not about to let you down. Rest assured that no matter what the immediate outcome, your future is completely in His hands.

---

[54] *Moody Monthly*, April 1990, 76 as quoted in www.bible.org.

2. Pray for God's guidance and protection.

Perhaps nothing makes a pastor feel more desperate than being relentlessly badgered by unappeasable church members. Just remember that when you don't know what to do, God always does, and will tell you if you'll ask Him. James 1:5 says that whenever you ask for wisdom, He will give it every time.

God has never said, "Wow, that's a tough problem. Sorry, but I really don't know what to tell you." If you will seek Him, He will download His wisdom from heaven and will instruct you concerning what to do.

God's wisdom tells us that the real enemy we fight goes beyond the man or woman screaming and shaking his or her finger in your face. You're involved in spiritual warfare, so you must use spiritual weapons to fight this conflict. Paul said, "For the weapons of our warfare are not carnal but mighty in God for pulling down strongholds" (2 Cor 10:4 NKJV).

Prayer is the key to victory. Ask the intercessors in your church to join you in praying against the demonic attacks. Only then can you move forward in hopeful assurance that God's will is being accomplished in His way.

3. Make sure you're fulfilling all duties on your job description.

A church is *not* being abusive if they fire the pastor who operates as a dictator instead of a shepherd. God instructs His leaders to be "examples to the flock." Pastors who look at pornography on the Internet, or are involved in inappropriate relationships, need to voluntarily step down and receive counseling.

We also know that some ministers are lazy. Congregations have every right to fire you if you're slacking off your responsibilities and not doing your job. One small-town pastor received criticism because he hadn't visited the shut-ins for over a year. The solution goes without saying—go visit the shut-ins!

If you expect your flock to faithfully follow, you must also be faithful to fulfill all duties on your job description. And do it with *excellence*. "Whatever you do, do your work heartily, as for the Lord rather than for men" (Col. 3:23).

Are you diligent in Bible study, prayer, and sermon preparation? Are you burdened for the lost with a plan to reach them? Or, are you lazy, contentious, and overly abrasive? Be sure that you're doing everything possible on your end to fulfill your pastoral duties, which makes you deserving of your earnings. "For the Scripture says, 'You shall not muzzle the ox while he is threshing,' and 'The laborer is worthy of his wages'" (1 Tim. 5:18 NAS).

4. Be above reproach in integrity.
When Paul faced false accusations from the Pharisees, he looked at the Council without blinking and said, "Brethren, I have lived my life with a perfectly good conscience before God up to this day" (Acts 23:1). Peter adds: "And keep a good conscience so that in the thing in which you are slandered, those who revile your good behavior in Christ may be put to shame. For it is better, if God should will it so, that you suffer for doing what is right rather than for doing what is wrong" (1 Pet. 3:16-17). Keeping a clear conscience is a powerful defense against accusations being hurled at you.

The most important question is not, "Who's in charge of this church?" but "Who's in charge of my heart?" Jesus said, "Blessed are the pure in heart" (Matt. 5:8). A good prayer during this time would be: "Lord, I want to behave like You because I want to glorify Your name."

Are you doing anything morally wrong? First Timothy 3:2 says that an overseer must be "above reproach" and "respectable." Pastors who have experienced moral failure should step down from the pulpit and seek help. If you are doing anything to disqualify you from serving, you must ask forgiveness and do what is necessary to make restitution.

Remember the Lord is in the restoration business. Repentant confession is the first and most necessary step you can take. "If we confess our sins, He is faithful and just to forgive us our sins and to cleanse us from all unrighteousness" (1 John 1:9 NKJV).

Don't wait. Do it now!

5. Don't let the church bullies intimidate you.
Pastor abusers grow in confidence if they sense that you're afraid of them. You must stand strong in the Lord if you're going to win this battle.

In the early 1950's, Jerry Collins got the job of his dreams. He earned twenty-five cents for fetching every baseball that had been knocked out of the minor league ballpark where he worked. He couldn't have been happier—until the day the neighborhood bully stopped him.

Holding up his fist, the ruffian demanded, "Give me your money, or else!" This terrified Jerry, but he wasn't about to surrender his earnings to this thug. However, he also knew that if he ran away, the bully would eventually hunt him down and threaten him again.

Just then, he remembered someone telling him that a hard, fast karate chop to the Adam's apple would make anyone cry. He hardly had time to think as this hooligan warned him one last time. Jerry flattened out his hand and quickly chopped him in the throat. Sure enough, the tough guy fell to his knees, clutching his throat and spitting!

With renewed confidence, Jerry stammered, "And, and, and you better not ever mess with me again!"

The bully never bothered him after that.

Years later, Jerry became a pastor, but never forgot this valuable lesson from his childhood about standing up to bullies.

If you are following the Lord Jesus, you're *going* to face some thugs, and you need to understand how to deal with them. Psychologist Robert M. Bramson writes: "Individuals behave in a difficult manner because they have learned that doing so keeps others off balance and incapable of effective action."[55]

Church bullies often try to frighten pastors into bowing down or running away. Don't let them scare you, but carry on with an air of confidence. When David confronted Goliath, God stood with him in a miraculous victory, just as He will throughout your battle. First Peter 3:14 is a reminder that persecution is a sign of God's blessing on you, and that you shouldn't feel intimidated by them: "But even if you should suffer for the sake of righteousness, you are blessed. And do not fear their intimidation, and do not be troubled."

A Southern Baptist pastor told us that the group that hated him offered him a severance package and asked him to resign on the coming Sunday. He had been at the church for a couple of years, and the same deacons had forced out the previous pastor in less than two years. The abusers gave him the impression that they represented the voices of the entire congregation. Here's what happened:

> That Sunday, the Director of Missions was present to moderate the meeting. The group that was against me thought I was going to resign.

---

[55] Bramson, Robert M. *Coping With Difficult People.* New York, NY: Ballantine Books, 1981, 5.

Instead, I got up and told the congregation, "I just want everyone to know that God called me to be the pastor of this church and I'm not leaving!"

As soon as I said that, the majority of the congregation got up and gave me a standing ovation. Those who opposed me sat there with shocked looks on their faces. At the moment they knew they had lost their fight against me. They had made me think they were in the majority, but it turned out they were only a small group.

They all quit the church that day and have never come back. They had made my life miserable, but after they left, the strife stopped. It's so good to have peace in the church again!

6. Seek the counsel of pastors who have confronted their abusers. You need to find some "lifelines"—spiritual veterans who can counsel you in the presence of your enemies. You can gain a wealth of wisdom by listening to pastors who have already battled with wolves. Standing alone when surprised by antagonists may seem convenient, but it is foolish and dangerous. "The way of a fool is right in his own eyes, but a wise man is he who listens to counsel" (Prov. 12:15).

Seeking godly advice from several different points of view will help you sort out your options. Learn from their experiences, and ask them how they would handle your situation. "For by wise guidance you will wage war, and in abundance of counselors there is victory" (Prov. 24:6).

A word of caution. Denominational intermediaries over regions, such as Director of Missions or District Superintendents, tend to be loyal to the abusive church instead of the abused shepherd. Some of them actually prescribe policies viewing pastors as temporary and church boards as permanent. Lloyd Rediger states: "Denominational officers often have little power or inclination to rescue pastors when they come under serious attack . . . (and) may even collude in their destruction."[56]

One pastor we interviewed was shocked by the lack of support he received from a representative of his denomination:

> We called a meeting of the entire congregation and the Superintendent from our denomination also attended. Immediately the controllers got up and start telling lies about me. The Superintendent knew they were lying, but he sat there in silence and never confronted them.

---

[56] Rediger, 135.

After the meeting, I told the Superintendent, "Just a week ago you told our church council that what they were doing to me was evil. Then tonight as that group got up and told lies about me, you never said a word. I had to defend myself alone. You never even tried to help me."

His response was, "I have to rescue the church, not you."

Hopefully you have a good relationship with your denominational representative, but don't be surprised if he isn't as sympathetic to you as you might expect. Since his financial support is generally derived from the church, your pleas for help may be drowned out by the demands of those who pay him. He knows that after you are gone, he must still maintain a relationship with the church that abused you, and he doesn't want to be on sour terms with them.

However, if he is favorable toward you, he might be able to help you receive a better severance package from the church. He may also help you find a new place to minister.

7. Seek a faithful friend to confide in.

As if pastor abuse isn't bad enough, it's made worse if you must endure the attacks alone. However, sharing every hurt feeling with your wife could be more than she needs to hear. Counselor Barney Self revealed that pastor's wives are often "wounded more deeply than the ministers (because) the wife can't talk to anybody. She can't talk to her friends because her friends are still at church; she can't talk to her co-workers because if they are not a part of her church, she doesn't want to throw rocks at her church."[57]

Instead of dumping your frustrations on your spouse's overly burdened shoulders, find a caring friend who will listen to your troubles while protecting your confidence. The operative word here is *protecting*. Proverbs 17:17 reminds us of a welcome truth for those who suffer: "A friend loves at all times, and a brother is born for adversity." Being able to vent to a trusted friend can help lift the weight off your soul. "Bear one another's burdens, and thus fulfill the law of Christ" (Gal. 6:2).

We must warn you to be extremely careful about the person to whom you bear your soul. It's not uncommon for the so-called friend to turn into a betrayer. Pastor abusers know your confidants, and will

---

[57] Barney Self as quoted from www.baptistpress.org/bpnews.asp?ID=13358.

often extract "useable" information from them. Satan chose Eve, the closest to Adam, as the vehicle to bring about his downfall. With this in mind, make sure that you use wisdom in choosing your sounding board.

8. Forgive those who have hurt you.

No doubt, those who hate you can hurt you beyond words. It goes without saying that unforgiveness will do more to ruin your life and ministry than it will those who wounded you. Remember that in God's kingdom, forgiveness is not an elective curriculum but a required course.

Whenever you're involved in spiritual warfare, the enemy will attack through the chinks in your armor. You may never understand why those who called you as pastor have turned against you. It's beyond your comprehension how someone claiming to be a Christian can act so viciously, while supposedly "worshipping" the Lord every Sunday. Nevertheless, they do, which leaves you with a choice of how to deal with it.

In his book *Lee: The Last Years,* Charles Bracelen Flood reports that after the Civil War, Robert E. Lee visited a Kentucky lady who took him to the remains of a grand old tree in front of her house. There she bitterly cried that its limbs and trunk had been destroyed by Federal artillery fire. She looked to Lee for a word condemning the North or at least sympathizing with her loss.

After a brief silence, Lee said, "Cut it down, my dear Madam, and forget it."[58] It is better to let go of injustices than to allow bitterness to take root and poison the rest of your life. Forgiveness is necessary if you wish to move past the quagmire of inner pain that haunts your memory with the finesse of a bullhorn.

Injustices never make sense, but don't let their wrongdoings incite you to react improperly. Unforgiveness will cause a deeper wound to your heart than the ruthless attacks of the perpetrator. Remember that the Lord Jesus died for all sins, including the hateful assaults that have been spewed upon you.

Author Max Lucado has said, "You will never forgive anyone more than God has already forgiven you." Just as Stephen forgave those who were killing him, you must do the same. In all honesty, forgiveness isn't

---

[58] Michael Williams as quoted from www.sermonillustrations.com/a-z/f/forgiveness.htm.

for them; it's for you—to keep your heart pure so that God can continue to bless you. "Who may ascend into the hill of the LORD? Or who may stand in His holy place? He who has clean hands and a pure heart" (Ps. 24:3-4 NKJV).

9. Protect your spouse and children.

Lest you forget, your family is a higher priority in God's sight than the church. That's why you must manage your own household well *before* you take care of God's children (1 Tim. 3:5). What does it profit a pastor to win the congregation's approval and lose his family?

The innocent, unnoticed victims of pastor abuse are the members of the minister's household. One terminated pastor shared how church turmoil can affect the family:

> These attacks are made in the open against you. Your wife hears about it in the community, and the children pick it up at school. It can be very devastating for them.[59]

It's of utmost importance to keep your family's relationship with the Lord separated from the church abuse. One of the most loving things you can do for your wife and children is to protect them from the ungodly accusations and terrorist threats you are receiving.

PKs, or preacher's kids, didn't choose to be born in a glass house with unreal expectations. Even when raised by loving and godly parents, they can turn away from the faith if they witness church wolves attacking their father. All their years of learning in Sunday school can be negated by the hypocrisy of a handful of tyrants in one fell swoop. After reaching adulthood, they may completely withdraw from church, and it may take years before they even consider attending again. A former pastor told us:

> After the morning service, two elders' wives were standing in the hall, ripping me to shreds. My ten-year old daughter was standing right there and heard every bit of it. She came running to her mother crying. My wife asked what was wrong. She said, "Why do those ladies hate my daddy so much?"

---

[59] Marv Knox.

A wife can be crushed as she watches the attackers mercilessly pounce on her husband. One abused pastor's wife said she gets nauseous just thinking about church. Although she has maintained a close devotional life with the Lord, she views church more like vain religious activities that may, or may not, touch God's heart.

To the best of your ability, you must guard your wife and children from specific details regarding church problems. Children never need to know any of the politics going on in church, and wives don't need to know the gory details.

10. Don't take your own revenge, but leave vengeance to God.
James says, "For the anger of man does not achieve the righteousness of God" (James 1:20). Human retaliation never produces godly justice. It merely reveals an ugly flaw that the enemy will invariably use as a weapon against *you*.

C.S. Lewis once quipped, "Surely what a man does when he is taken off his guard is the best evidence for what sort of man he is. If there are rats in a cellar, you are most likely to see them if you go in very suddenly. But the suddenness does not create the rats; it only prevents them from hiding. In the same way, the suddenness of the provocation does not make me ill-tempered; it only shows me what an ill-tempered man I am."[60]

When your enemies slander you, it's natural to retaliate. However, acting on your impulses could destroy your testimony. Pause to listen to the inner voice of God's reason, and refuse to fight back. When Jesus was assaulted, "He did not revile in return; while suffering He uttered no threats, but kept entrusting Himself to Him who judges righteously" (1 Pet. 2:23). Sudden, unprovoked attacks are cheap shots. Although it's tempting to repay those who treat you wickedly, to recompense evildoers is God's prerogative alone. "Vengeance is Mine, I will repay," says the Lord (Rom. 12:19).

Rather than fighting back, Paul handed his persecutors over to the Lord. "Alexander the coppersmith did me much harm; the Lord will repay him according to his deeds" (2 Tim. 4:14). He was confident in knowing that God's justice is never wrong, while man's is often inappropriate. The Apostle placed his accuser in the Lord's hands, knowing that He would indeed settle the score. In light of the coming

---

[60] C.S. Lewis as quoted from www.quotedb.com.

Judgment, never forget the importance of doing the same. "So then each one of us shall give an account of himself to God" (Rom. 14:12).

11. View attacks for what they are—persecution.

If you've been faithful to God's calling and haven't done anything wrong, it's imperative that you view the slander and character assassination against you as groundless, godless persecution. We typically define persecution as something that occurs *outside* the church, such as unbelievers attacking and murdering Christians in a foreign country. However, pastor abuse is persecution *inside* the church. Nevertheless, although the persecution is not as severe as in other parts of the world, it's just as real.

God is allowing this fiery trial to refine you to produce a deeper spiritual work in your life. You've drawn closer to Him than ever before, and you've gained insight into truths that you've never grasped until now. For the first time in your life, you feel the painful loneliness and sting of rejection our Savior experienced from His abusers. Congratulations! You're experiencing a realm that few people know. You've now entered into "the fellowship of His sufferings" (Phil. 3:10).

To recompense those who are suffering for Him, Jesus promised a huge eternal reward. "Blessed are you when they revile and persecute you, and say all kinds of evil against you falsely for My sake. Rejoice and be exceedingly glad, for great is your reward in heaven, for so they persecuted the prophets who were before you" (Matthew 5:11-12 NKJV).

For this reason, viewing pastor abuse as persecution *leading to reward* will alter your perspective so you can see your trial in a positive light. When the apostles were unjustly flogged, they stayed optimistic and went on their way "rejoicing that they had been considered worthy to suffer shame for His name" (Acts 5:41). Rather than focusing on their persecutors, they fixed their eyes on their Savior and considered it an honor to suffer for Him.

If you'll choose to see His smiling face rather than their frowning faces, you will find yourself rejoicing in the midst of the battle.

12. Understand that you can't please everyone.

A former president was reported to have conducted polls before he would take a stand on certain issues. The outcome of the surveys often determined his political views. God didn't call you to be a politician, but His spokesman. You'll never survive in ministry if you strive to be a people-pleaser who takes more stock in public opinion than in God's Word.

People-pleasing is when we elevate the *second* greatest commandment to "love your neighbor," over the *greatest* commandment, "'You shall love the Lord your God with all your heart, and with all your soul, and with all your mind'" (Matt. 22:37). Fear of man displaces the fear of God and leads to disobedience.

We're not suggesting you become contentious. Do what you can, within limits, to keep from offending others. But always remember that the only poll you need to consult is the Lord's. Our ambition is to please the Lord of Glory above everyone else.

Paul said, "For am I now seeking the favor of men or of God? Or am I striving to please men? If I were still trying to please men, I would not be a bond-servant of Christ" (Gal. 1:10). We'll never go wrong if we use God's Instruction Book as our only immutable source to anchor our thoughts and opinions.

13. Make an attempt to be at peace with those who dislike you.
In his book, *Facing Unresolved Conflicts,* author Dr. Mario Rivera writes: "Disagreement can be an unpleasant word, but it is a realistic one . . . Christians don't necessarily have to agree. A church is not healthy just because everyone says 'yes.' A church is healthy when people begin to respect the rights of others to disagree with them, and they're free to express their own views."[61]

Church conflict not only produces chaos, but also rudely awakens us to the fact that some people will never reconcile. Still, it is incumbent upon us to try to be at peace. Scripture insists, "If possible so far as it depends on you, be at peace with all men" (Rom. 12:18). It may not be possible, but we must at least make an attempt.

Too often we want the offender to make the first move; to see his heart change before we make an attempt to resolve differences. But we must not focus our attention on the attacker's bitter attitude, waiting to see his or her repentance. Our main concern is to please the Lord. God will always bless the person who humbly initiates the conciliatory effort, even when you don't feel like it.

Peacemaking is one of the fundamentals of our faith. "Blessed are the peacemakers, for they shall be called the children of God" (Matt.

---

[61] Mario E. Rivera, *Facing Unresolved Conflicts,* Green Forrest, AR: New Leaf Press, 1998, 142.

5:9). Although difficult to swallow in one sitting, steps toward reconciliation can be taken if you're willing to try them. For example, your peacemaking mission might begin by simply shaking that person's hand with a smile on your face. Ask God for ideas, and He will give them to you. Even if that individual's heart doesn't melt in repentance, you can keep a clear conscience before God that you walked the high road of obedience.

14. Build a coalition of supportive leaders and laity who will speak up for you.

We're amazed at how many pastors have told us that it's only a small, vocal group who cause the trouble. As unbelievable as it may seem, pastor abusers usually don't represent the views of the majority. However, they're vocal, organized, and extremely vicious. Although most church members would say they support their pastor, they are usually silent, unorganized, and wimps. If you want to remain in your church, you must rally your supportive leaders and laity, and strongly encourage them to speak up. If the majority would take a stand, they will outnumber the critics.

Police officers can't keep society safe unless they arrest lawbreakers. Without policemen doing their jobs, the streets would be filled with renegades, robbing and raping innocent people. Imagine the anarchy that would ensue if only one law officer was responsible for arresting all crooks in an entire city. That's why it's called a police *force*, because they're united together to fight evil. If an officer is pursuing a dangerous criminal, he will call for "backup" so that he's not standing alone.

In too many instances, the pastor stands alone to fend off these beasts by himself. It doesn't have to be that way, if you'll call for a backup from your supporters. A pastor can weather almost any storm if he has the church leadership standing with him. A plurality of godly leadership acting as "a police force" can unite against religious rebels and prevent them from commandeering the church and running you off.

A pastor of a large church survived the onslaught because his elders stood with him. He told us:

> You wouldn't believe how many people beat me up after I came here. I survived their attacks because the elders took a stand to support me. I'm now in my third year here. The congregation is now united, we've

started a building project, and we're set to grow for the future. But none of that would have happened if the elders hadn't stood with me when I was under attack.

The church survived because its leadership was united. A chain is only as strong as its weakest link, so pastor abusers will try to exploit the weakest leader. It's usually a person with a flimsy backbone, who wants to be known as a peacemaker—but ignores the spirit of rebellion in the antagonists. All it takes to break up a united front is for one leader to work independently from the rest and give a sympathetic ear to the rebels. Kenneth Haugk writes:

> Church staff and lay leaders must maintain a united front, with no room for backbiting or unhealthy friction. An antagonist will discover such unhealthy conflict among leaders and use it. A united front does not mean agreement on all things, but mutual respect and support of others in their roles. This frustrates antagonists, who attempt to "divide and conquer."[62]

Sometimes all that's necessary to rally your supporters is for one influential church member to speak up for the pastor. When others see that happen, they'll gain the courage to also step forward. When the majority speaks up in your defense, the minority opposing you will shut up.

Jackie Robinson was the first black athlete to play major league baseball. Breaking baseball's color barrier, he faced jeering crowds in every stadium. While playing one day in his home stadium in Brooklyn, he committed an error. The fans began to ridicule him. He stood at second base, humiliated, while the fans jeered. Then, shortstop Pee Wee Reese came over and stood next to him. He put his arm around Jackie Robinson and faced the crowd. The fans grew quiet. Robinson later said that arm around his shoulder saved his career.[63]

It took courage for Pee Wee to stand up against the taunting of the crowd. Yet, his unwavering endorsement of Robinson silenced the hecklers and encouraged Jackie. Imagine what this could do for you.

---

[62] Haugk, 96.
[63] *Leadership* magazine as quoted from www.sermonillustrations.com/a-z/f/friendship.htm.

15. Install godly individuals into leadership.

John Maxwell has said, "Everything rises and falls on leadership." The solution to your pastor abuse situation might not be to change churches, but to change your church leadership. As we have already discussed in the preceding chapter, make every effort to close the loophole that pastor abusers use to grab power.

Installing godly leaders needs to occur before your conflict begins to *prevent* pastor abuse from happening. After the onslaught begins, it may be too late. However in your situation, replacing the ringleader with a compassionate member might be an option to consider.

If your congregation is ruled by elders, you will need to appeal your case to the board. If your church employs congregational vote, you must build a case that the rebellious abusers are committing mutiny against the pastor and must be held accountable. Then call for a vote to expel the abusers instead of letting them run you out of the church.

16. Bring in an outside mediator that both sides trust.

If you cannot solve the conflict from within your church, finding an outside mediator might be helpful. A negotiator that's not a church member could bring peace and stability to your troubled congregation. Although this sounds great on paper, it's extremely tough to implement if stubborn hearts and hot heads prevail. However, if you can find a go-between that both sides trust, a plan of action can be followed for each one involved.

The mediator will serve in an advisory capacity by listening and sharing the needs, ideas, and concerns held by both the congregation and the pastor. This peacemaker will always operate in an atmosphere of strict confidentiality and trust, seeking the promotion of constructive and caring communications between the pastor and those who are at odds with him.

This intermediary can aid in these ways:

1. Assist in understanding the roles and expectations of both sides.

2. Provide a bridge of communication for loving, honest and confidential discussion.

3. Help the pastor and church deal with conflict by fairly weighing each side of the issues according to Scripture.

4. Write down a plan of action that each party can take to resolve their differences.

5. Evaluate and monitor the follow-through of each party.

The above actions will only work if everyone is willing to place their issues on the altar in a spirit of cooperation. Conflict-resolution will never work unless every person is sensitive to the leading of the Holy Spirit.

17. Combat gossipers by exposing them publicly.

For weeks, primetime television featured a program my wife and I fell in love with called "The Mole."[64] It was quite intellectually challenging, as each week one paid disrupter would secretly undermine the work of the other contestants who were competing to win a large cash prize. The only way they could escape weekly elimination was to accurately answer questions to uncover the identity of the mole.

That show, in some respects, is a perfect picture of what pastors face every time they are publicly or privately accused through slander and gossip. Some time ago I was approached by a friend I hadn't seen in almost a year. It seems he had heard some things about me from one of the brethren, who had heard it from someone else, and so on. I was shocked how the facts had been so grossly perverted, so I asked who told him. "Ah, well, I'd rather not say," he stammered.

Why do we protect gossips? They pass out evil reports, demeaning lies, or at best, half-truths, and then bask in an unbiblical code of secrecy. Proverbs 20:19 says, "He who goes about as a slanderer reveals secrets, *therefore do not associate with a gossip*." Do Christians think that covering up the slanderous source is somehow virtuous?

Those who spread slander and strife among the brethren are on the list of seven things that are an abomination to God: "There are six things which the Lord hates, yes, seven which are an abomination to Him . . . A false witness who utters lies, and one who spreads strife among brothers" (Prov. 6:16, 19). If God detests these evil people, why are church members so willing to accept their malicious gossip and then protect their identities? Satan disseminates his most wicked attacks in secrecy and some Christians are all too willing to assist him.

The biblical solution to the gossip dilemma is to expose them publicly.

> And do not participate in the unfruitful deeds of darkness, *but instead even expose them*; for it is disgraceful even to speak of the things which are done by them in secret. But all things become

---

[64] Pastor Mike Johnston

visible when they are exposed by the light, for everything that becomes visible is light" (Eph. 5:11-13).

Although you might think openly reprimanding them is unloving, the early church publicly rebuked those causing strife and turmoil. Paul didn't cover up the actions of the heinous Hymenaeus (1 Tim. 1:19-20), the attacker Alexander (2 Tim. 4:14), or the deserter Demas (2 Tim 4:10). John, who is known as the loving disciple, called public attention to despicable Diotrephes (3 John 9). Furthermore, Paul gave this bold command to the elders: "Those who continue in sin, *rebuke in the presence of all, so that the rest also may be fearful* of sinning (1 Tim. 5:20).

18. Exercise church discipline when necessary.

It's amazing how one argumentative person can generate a dark cloud of division and discontentment over an entire church. But they do. Although you might like to duck the issue, the Bible tells us what to do. Remove the one causing strife, and your trouble will go out the door with him. "For lack of wood the fire goes out, and where there is no whisperer, contention quiets down. Like charcoal to hot embers and wood to fire, so is a contentious man to kindle strife" (Prov. 26:20-21).

If a ringleader causes the abuse, follow the steps mentioned in Titus 3:10: "Reject a factious man after a first or second warning." The importance of church discipline has been discussed in the previous chapter, and we'll give you some advice in the next chapter as well.

19. Buy your time and carefully do your homework before running to another church.

If things are getting worse rather than better, buy some time so you can look for another church or vocation. Continue to serve and minister as best you can under the circumstances, and maintain close ties with the Lord. If God leads, start looking for other opportunities, but not with a church that has a history of pastor abuse. Do your homework. Ask questions about the church or vocation *before* mailing your resume.

You shouldn't run away from your responsibilities just to get relief. You might be jumping out of the frying pan into the fire! I'll talk more about how to look for another church in the final chapter. However, sometimes you'll be forced out before another door opens. If that's your situation, pay close attention to the next point.

20. Before the abusers force you to resign, negotiate a severance package.

When a reality check indicates that staying at the church isn't a wise choice, the advice from one abused pastor will help to cushion your departure. His only two options were to either fight the troublemakers who controlled the church or resign. (This may be your only two choices, as well.) He was confident most of his congregation supported him, but he also realized how extremely difficult it would be to dethrone the long-standing coalition of deacons that were fighting him.

Realizing that combating the controllers would take a toll on his family, he offered to step aside with one stipulation—that they would provide him with six months of severance pay and insurance. If not, he would call for a congregational vote, which the abusers didn't want, so they gave him his request. Instead of having to scramble to find another job, this safety net allowed him some time to seek another ministry.

Before you resign without an income, make sure you acquire a severance package that will give you a financial cushion while you are looking for another opportunity. The following simple steps should be incorporated in your plan as you proceed.

First, try to find someone who will represent your best interests to the committee. This negotiator can be someone outside the congregation, such as a Director of Missions, District Superintendent, or a local pastor, as long as they are influential and acceptable to both sides.

Next, if you've done nothing to warrant being terminated, try to get six months salary and insurance. Remind them that many churches often take over a year to search for a replacement, so six months' severance pay isn't unreasonable. If they refuse to listen to your request, try for five months, then four. Don't settle for less than three months salary and insurance.

They'll probably try to attach strings to your agreement such as: "If we hear that you are talking to church members, we will cut off your support." Be careful about signing such an agreement, since the terms are based on hearsay. It's likely that someone who hates you will claim that you're dividing the church, and will push to cut off your severance pay. Do your best to keep your severance pay free from conditions and loopholes. Make sure the agreement is signed by you, the negotiator, and the church representative, and that everyone receives a copy.

Finally, in lieu of getting nothing, acquire what you can. Sadly, 59% of terminated pastors are given no severance package by the callous churches that oust them.[65] With this statistic in mind, it's better to get something rather than nothing. It's tragic that a church can hire a pastor and then coldheartedly toss him and his family out on the street empty-handed.

Another option to consider is to "transition out" of the church. See if you can work out a deal with those opposing you to let you send out your resume for six months as you continue to pastor. The understanding is that you will be actively looking for another congregation and won't be terminated during that period. If you don't find a church during that time, you will resign and the church will give you a three month severance package.

This will give you time to look without having "terminated" written on your resume. It will also let the church know you will be gone within the time period. Put it in writing with both parties' signatures. If you find another church before then, they will not be obligated to pay your severance package.

21. Final resort—Leave the church.

Because each situation is different, there is no textbook answer for the proper way to leave a church. Some pastors exit after delivering a scathing, bold message of rebuke, which certainly has scriptural support. Other pastors take a more gentle approach, leaving with their dignity intact, without causing a disturbance. When the minister takes the high road, the abusers are often exposed as the bad guys who ran him off.

However, you do well to remember that the antagonists who remain in the church after your departure usually have the final word with congregants. Studies show that two-thirds of churches will not reveal the truth regarding the forced exit.[66] Nevertheless, by employing the second approach, the pastor doesn't look like the tyrant the bullies made him out to be.

After leaving, the great temptation is to keep looking back. Rather than doing that, shake the dust of your feet and look forward to all that God has in store for you. We can tell you from personal experience

---

[65] John C. LaRue. "Forced Exits: High-Risk Churches" *Your Church,* May/June 1996, as quoted in www.christianitytoday.com.
[66] ibid.

that your new adventure will be far better than your experience in your abusive church. Start rejoicing, knowing that better days are yet to come.

"Now, dear brothers and sisters, I am still not all I should be, but I am focusing all my energies on this one thing: Forgetting the past and looking forward to what lies ahead, I strain to reach the end of the race and receive the prize for which God, through Christ Jesus, is calling us up to heaven" (Phil. 3:13-14 NLT).

Chapter 11

Showdown with the Abusers

Drive out the scoffer, and contention will go out, even strife and dishonor will cease. (Prov. 22:10)

In an episode of *The Andy Griffith Show*, a couple of farmers had parked their truck along the roadside, illegally selling their vegetables. When Deputy Barney Fife spotted these law-breakers, he pulled his squad car over and told them they had to leave. The two big bullies stood up to him, saying they weren't going anywhere. Overcome with fear and trembling, a shaky Barney ran back to his car and sped away.

After returning to the courthouse, deputy Fife fidgeted nervously, fearful of having to confront the lawbreakers again. When Sheriff Andy found out what the farmers had done, he reminded Barney that he was an officer of the law, and he had to go back and order them to get out of town.

Barney reluctantly returned to the veggie stand and asked them again to leave. The thugs walked up, stood in front of him, and defiantly crossed their arms. Looking them in the eye, he tapped on his badge and said, "Sure you guys are big, but this badge represents people who are a lot bigger than you are. Now, are you going to leave?" The bullies backed down, loaded up their truck and drove away.

We can learn a few things from Barney Fife when it comes to handling church bullies. The troublemakers, who have usurped authority, are trying to intimidate you. Despite your warnings, they refuse to leave. Now is the time to remember your divine calling. You have been "deputized" by the King of kings to maintain order in His church, and the spiritual badge you're wearing represents a God who is much bigger than those pipsqueaks.

Although you might be tempted to throw up your hands and leave, you mustn't flee the premises just yet. God *may* lead you to leave later, but He has an important job for you to do first. You must look the bullies in the eye and tap your badge. Unless someone unseats the abusers who control the church, they'll run off every future pastor who doesn't bow down and kiss their feet.

Jesus told us to be both wise and innocent in our dealings with others: "Behold, I send you forth as sheep in the midst of wolves: be ye therefore wise as serpents, and harmless as doves" (Matt. 10:16). "Wisdom" refers to the proper strategy to employ, while "harmless" signifies having a calm spirit that refuses to retaliate when attacked. In contrast, your abusers are as wise as doves, and as harmful as serpents. Don't let their insensitive and ignorant comments confound you, or their hateful spirits to incite you to strike back.

When your attempts to appease them aren't working, wisdom dictates that you must change your strategy. Your situation isn't going to get any better with more one-on-one coffee chats. The people you're dealing with are rebellious people who are slanderers, backbiters, and gossipers—and they will continually create strife until they're held accountable, ejected from the church, or stomp out on their own.

God told Jeremiah, "See, I have appointed you this day over the nations and over the kingdoms, *to pluck up and to break down, to destroy and to overthrow*, to build and to plant." (Jer. 1:10). Before he could build and plant, he first had to tear down and overthrow the unbiblical systems and ungodly attitudes.

The Lord often calls His servants to the same task as Jeremiah. As pastors begin the process of renewing the church, they will receive opposition from those who want to protect strongholds that God says to "pluck up" and "overthrow." This clash of mindsets will ultimately lead to a major confrontation with the abusers.

Winning the Battle

You're probably wondering, *Can I win the battle against the abusers?* Most certainly, but a few pieces must be in place.

First, confronting clergy abusers is one of the higher levels of spiritual warfare, so you must carefully follow the Lord's leading. Pride can tempt you to engage in battles you're not called to fight, and fear can cause you to run from confrontations the Lord wants you to face. You must know whether He's telling you to keep standing your ground, or if it's time to move on to your next assignment. You may want to ask yourself, *If the entire ecclesiastical system is corrupt, why would I want to stay in that?* There really isn't a textbook answer, nor is there a scripted battle plan since every situation is different. My pastoral interviews lead me to believe that God directs some to leave and others to remain. Only the Holy Spirit can guide you in this decision.

Second, you must have the majority of your board and/or congregation supporting you. Without this show of confidence, the Lord's work will be hampered or halted. One pastor told us he had a large majority of his congregation firmly behind him, but most of the deacons against him. Although he was willing to stay and fight the battle, the Lord told him to leave. He knew that if he didn't have strong support from his deacons, they would keep resisting his leadership and matters would only get worse. However, if you have the majority of leaders on your side, it's likely that you will prevail.

Third, remember Esther's courageous words as she risked her life to do what was right, "If I perish, I perish" (Esther 4:16). If your leaders and flock rally behind you and the abusers leave the church, you win. In the event that you're fired, you *still win*—if you have obeyed what the Lord instructed you to do. As we've stated throughout this book, stiff-necked religious leaders have always persecuted the Lord's messengers. Having a successful ministry isn't defined by winning a church fight, but by carrying out the Lord's will. Trust Him for victory regardless of the outcome.

Confronting the Trouble

So when should they be dealt with? As soon as their schemes are discovered, and not a moment later. It will only get worse if you wait too long. Confrontation is never easy, but is always necessary.

The apostle John is known as "the apostle of love," and yet he was not without his church troublemakers. Sometimes one wonders which was worse for him; being boiled in oil, or dealing with the antagonistic Diotrephes (let's call him iDiot). If you have one of these aggressively hostile controllers in your congregation, you know just what we're talking about. John had this to say about iDiot:

> I wrote something to the church; but Diotrephes, *who loves to be first among them*, does not accept what we say. For this reason, if I come, *I will call attention to his deeds which he does*, unjustly accusing us with wicked words; and not satisfied with this, neither does he himself receive the brethren, and he forbids those who desire to do so, and *puts them out of the church* (3 John 9-10).

Obviously, iDiot was a well-established church leader who loved being in charge, had slandered John using "wicked words," and had a history of driving God's servants out of the church. (Can you see how their methods haven't changed in two thousand years?) As pastor abusers always do, he gained an audience and was passing around false rumors about John, hoping to discredit the apostle's authority. Whenever someone like this controls a church, it's amazing how many people will acquiesce to him.

Because every pastor abuse scenario varies, I can't give you a precise step-by-step list concerning the exact measures to take. However, I can propose some ideas that will help you mobilize your forces and point you in the right direction. If you ask for God's wisdom, the Holy Spirit will lead you concerning how to proceed.

1. Rally your leaders to stand with you.

The tyrants you are dealing with must be confronted about their unacceptable behavior, or the troubles they cause will never end. It's unwise to fight this battle alone, so first bring together your supportive leaders who will defend your authority. If you haven't assembled this group before the showdown, you'll find yourself outnumbered, outlasted, and outside.

Your trusted leaders need to go along with you to visit with the angry person or group. Not only do they show the abusers a "united front," you also need them as witnesses to back up everything that has been said in the meeting. The troublemakers need to see that you have the support of respected leaders standing at your side, which will deter them from distorting what you said during the skirmish.

2. Instruct your prayer warriors to intercede for you.

Ask a group of prayer-warriors to intercede for you through the crisis. Prayer opens communication with God, and invokes Him to intervene in your situation. When I was ready to embark on one difficult meeting with our "angry controller," I invited my prayer group into my living room.[67] We prayed that God would direct the meeting, that I would not retaliate, that my behavior would reflect the character of Christ, and that God's will would be accomplished. I went into that meeting with trusted leaders by my side and our warriors on their knees in my house, covering us all with prayer. I can't imagine what the outcome would

---

[67] Pastor Mike Johnston

have been if I had confronted them without this spiritual shield of protection.

3. Keep ministering to the other sheep.
In the time you have left before the showdown, keep ministering to the rest of your flock in as many ways as you can. This will not only get your mind off of your own needs, but will reinforce in your members' minds that you *are* doing your job, which the angry group claims you are not doing. "Be diligent to know the state of your flocks, and attend to your herds" (Prov. 27:23 NKJV).

Pray for the sheep you are visiting. Serve them. Love them. Protect them. Do everything you can to keep them out of harm's way. You may actually request that some individuals in your flock *not* attend to the showdown meeting, since they could be crushed by some of the things that are said.

However, don't visit members' homes to discuss the conflict or to recruit an army. Go there to minister to their needs. Steer the conversation away from church disputes because what you say may be misinterpreted—and shared on the phone after you leave.

If you've been truly ministering to the rest of the flock, they will ultimately support you after the smoke clears. Don't count on them to speak up when the conflict escalates into a verbal shootout. They might be afraid to speak up in a public face-off because they've been bullied by these controllers for so long. However, after you've boldly declared the truth about their unacceptable behavior, the fearful flock will applaud the man of God who refused to bow down.

4. Don't retaliate in anger.
The most difficult assignment during the battle will be trying to maintain your composure when your angry adversaries begin hurling grenades at you. Remember this verse: "A hot-tempered man stirs up strife, but the slow to anger pacifies contention" (Prov. 15:18). You must not explode or become outraged, because it will make you appear out-of-control and defensive, which plays right into their hands. They'll point their fingers at your lack of control (while ignoring their own), and use it to impugn your integrity. That's why it is imperative for you to stay in an attitude of prayer during the confrontation, asking for strength not to retaliate. "He who guards his mouth and his tongue, guards his soul from troubles" (Prov. 21:23).

Paul instructed Timothy not to speak harshly to an older man or woman, but rather to appeal to them respectfully (1 Tim. 5:1-2). One pastor shared this bit of wisdom: "I kept picturing my own father (who was gentle and respectful) as I spoke to the angry man in our church. It kept me from blowing my stack and blowing the conflict completely out of proportion."

5. Establish the ground rules for the showdown.

Never allow the abusers to set the time and place where the battle will take place. Piranhas will always welcome you into their river. And like a football team, they psychologically feel invigorated when they have the home field advantage. That's why you should establish the time, place, and ground rules for every meeting with the opposing group.

If you allow them to control the meeting, it may well turn into a one-sided, hostile rampage against you, leaving you with no chance to respond. Establish the regulations at the beginning of the meeting so that everyone must abide by the same rules. A pastor shared this testimony:

> Before the final confrontation, I warned everyone that I wouldn't allow anyone in our congregation to disrespect other members. I had told the complainer that he could say what he wished, as long as it was done respectfully.
>
> When the meeting began, the hot-headed man immediately started reeling off falsehoods about innocent members of our congregation. I stopped him and called the church to prayer. That's where the battle was finally won. As the church prayed, the irate menace left the building fuming. We were finally free from his control. God took His church back that evening.

6. Guard your integrity and walk uprightly.

Battling with pastor abusers is never easy. (This kind will only come out with prayer and fasting.) But if you'll hang in there and keep speaking the truth in love, God can use you to free your church from those who have been controlling it for years. They think they own the church, but they don't. It belongs to God.

Always take the high road, especially when they hit you with a low blow. Regardless of the outcome, God will ultimately honor those who walk uprightly. David wrote: "Vindicate me, O Lord, for I have walked in my integrity; and I have trusted in the Lord without wavering" (Ps. 26:1). Don't forget that although Jesus was sinless, He still had skirmishes with those who controlled the synagogues. The fact that you're being attacked means you probably are doing what is right, and sharing in the fellowship of His sufferings. Place your situation completely in God's hands and keep saying to yourself, "The battle is the Lord's."

7. Remove the wicked from the fellowship.
Someone once said pastors should treat troublemakers like a farmer treats a stump in the field—you just plow around them. That may work in the field, but in the church it ain't gonna fly. Antagonists can draw crowds faster than a man throwing money out of a ten-story building. They'll rally church members around controversial issues, which ultimately creates friction and strife. It's just as wrong to permit these pests to control the church as it is to ignore vandals stealing the "Bridge is out" road sign.

Here's how the Bible tells us to handle these church vagabonds:

- **Recognize them.**
  First, you need to know who they are and what they're up to. They won't stand up in church and announce that they are the troublemakers. However, they will tell you in many other ways. Once you identify them, you need to keep a close eye on them. Although the faces change, the personalities are generally always the same.

  Paul warned the church in Rome: "I urge you, brothers, to watch out for those who cause divisions and put obstacles in your way that are contrary to the teaching you have learned. Keep away from them. For such people are not serving our Lord Christ, but their own appetites. By smooth talk and flattery they deceive the minds of naive people" (Rom. 16:17-18).

- **Rebuke them.**
  It's uncanny how these dissenters worm their way into influential positions on boards and committees. Once seated there, they consider their authority higher than the pastor, and are quick to demonstrate it. More often than not, these people are very intimidating, so the congregation would rather promote them than be a target of their wrath. However, since they disqualify

themselves through unholy actions and attitudes, they must be rebuked and dethroned.

Some pastors have mistakenly believed that if they will praise these renegades publicly their attacks will subside. According to Haugk, nothing is farther from the truth:

> Excessive praise involves two dangers: First, it raises an antagonist's view of himself or herself. Increasing the confidence of an antagonist feeds the emotional power base from which he or she will launch an attack on you or another leader. Second, by excessively praising antagonists in front of others, you make it easier for them to build a strong following. You will have accorded them special status.[68]

Instead of attempting to pacify malcontents over and over again, we should simply obey God's instructions: "Warn a divisive person once, and then warn him a second time. After that, have nothing to do with him. You may be sure that such a man is warped and sinful; he is self-condemned" (Titus 3:10-11).

- **Remove them.**

Several years ago, my son and I discovered that a rental property we owned had been infested with cockroaches.[69] This caused quite a stir with every tenant in the complex, so we needed to quickly extricate them from the premises.

In a foolish attempt to save money, we decided not to call an exterminator. Instead, we set up traps that didn't work. Then we sprayed the units, which only seemed to work as fertility hormones to help them multiply. We finally conceded and called a professional, who knew exactly how to get rid of them—and did.

One of the healthiest things that can happen to a church is to purge out its troublemakers. Paul told the church at Corinth not to play games with problematic people. In his vividly direct way, he told them to "remove the wicked man from among yourselves" (1 Cor. 5:13).

Although this sounds "unchristian" to some, church discipline is clearly mandated by God to keep unity in the church. It only takes a few contagious, negative people to spread their germs to an entire

---

[68] Haugk, 109.
[69] Pastor Mike Johnston

congregation. Again Paul says, "Do you not know that a little leaven leavens the whole lump of dough?" (1 Cor. 5:6).

Follow the principles explained in chapter eight concerning church discipline and removing rebellious members from the flock. The process should be explained in the bylaws of your church government.

When it's right to move on
Don't assume that just because God favors your position it will be an easy task. Most antagonists couldn't care less about the will of God, or the verses suggesting you do this or don't do that. Pastor abusers want to win at any cost. Second to that is they want you out!

The steps that's outlined above may not work if too many abusers are firmly established in control positions. They are entrenched in seats of power because timid congregations have given them their way, and they're usually too afraid to unseat them. And that leaves you with the only other option—leave the church and shake the dust off your feet.

When Jesus sent out His disciples to minister throughout Israel, He told them, "And whoever does not receive you, nor heed your words, as you go out of that house or that city, shake the dust of your feet" (Matt. 10:14). Sadly these words can be applied to many pastors in modern-day churches that are not received as God's messengers. He warned they will "scourge you in the synagogues" (Matt. 10:17). While refusing to admit wrong doing, these self-righteous religionists who claim to love God will persecute *in their houses of worship* the very prophets sent by the Lord Himself!

The Lord instructed the disciples further, "But whenever they persecute you in this city, *flee to the next . . .*" (Matt. 10:23). When the abusive church stubbornly refuses to accept what the Lord wants to accomplish in that congregation, what merit is there for a pastor staying? Jesus did not instruct His disciples to stay and fight, or hold their ground and yield to the persecution. He told them to pack up and move on.

Although some may view fleeing as cowardice, in reality it is exercising wise obedience to the Lord's command. The apostle Paul often escaped from those who wanted to kill him in order to shut down his ministry. Jesus instructed him to "make haste, and *get out of Jerusalem quickly*, because they will not accept your testimony about Me" (Acts 22:18). When pastor abusers conspire against you, He may lead you to take your ministry it to another place. Instead of carelessly exposing yourself to those who want to destroy you, it's wiser to relocate to where you will be received.

Now we understand His admonition to be "wise as serpents and harmless as doves" (Matt. 10:16). How are serpents wise? They don't unnecessarily expose themselves to bodily harm and can escape quickly when they're attacked. Yet when cornered, instead of striking back like a snake, we are to be as "harmless as doves." No dove has ever hurt anyone, and neither should we.

When all else fails, and you sense no purpose in staying until the last body is dragged out of the sanctuary, pack up and get out! Remember that your family comes before your church. You don't want to lose your wife over this, as many pastors have.

Lazarus Ministries offers some advice to pastors at this difficult crossroad: "One major mistake that pastors make is to stay in hopeless situations that result in his forced resignation or even a church split."[70]

There is a season for everything under heaven and this may well be the right time God wants you to make your exit. It's not your fault that the pastor search committee lied to you during the interview process, telling you what you wanted to hear, just to get their pulpit filled. Then after you move your family across the country to be their pastor, they tear you apart and run you off. God will hold them accountable.

Before you clean out your office desk, remember to acquire one very important document—a three to six month's severance package. It will be much better for your family to have a few months guaranteed salary than to leave the church empty-handed. Try starting at six months. Tell the abusers you're willing to leave, but you must have a signed agreement first. In all probability, the antagonists will grudgingly give in to your request, just to get rid of you. Then afterward, they'll brag to the congregation how extremely generous they were in compensating you.

After resigning, how long should you remain in the community? The consensus among experienced churchmen is not long. Donald Bubna said, "The sooner one leaves following the resignation, the sooner the healing begins and the church can start to look for a successor." (Pity the poor soul that follows you!)

In the next chapter, we'll examine four options to consider after leaving.

---

[70] Lazarus Ministries is a church conflict resolution ministry. www.lazarusministries.org

Chapter 12

Life After Leaving: What Do I Do Now?

"And as for you, you meant evil against me, but God meant it for good in order to bring about this present result . . ." (Gen. 50:20)

Do you feel like a failure because the pastor abusers drove you out of the church? Perhaps you think you "missed God" and made an enormous mistake by accepting the call to be their pastor.

Now is the time to review your situation from heaven's perspective. Perhaps you've overlooked this message that Jesus delivered to the Pharisees: "Behold, *I am sending you prophets* and wise men and scribes; some of them you will kill and crucify, and *some of them you will scourge in your synagogues, and persecute* from city to city" (Matt. 23:34).

God sent His prophets to preach to hard-hearted, rebellious people, even though He knew *beforehand* that His messengers would be rejected and persecuted. Read what God told Ezekiel:

> "And I am sending you to them who are stubborn and obstinate children; and you shall say to them, 'Thus says the Lord God.' As for them, whether they listen or not—for they are a rebellious house—they will know that a prophet has been among them. And you, son of man, neither fear them nor fear their words, though thistles and thorns are with you and you sit on scorpions; neither fear their words nor be dismayed at their presence, for they are a rebellious house. But you shall speak My words to them whether they listen or not, for they are rebellious." (Ezek. 2:4-7)

Did God's prophets make a mistake by going into a hostile environment and preaching to stubborn people? No.

Were they "failures" because they were mistreated? Of course not. And neither are you. There's no reason to be ashamed of being fired when you've obeyed what God sent you to do. Actually, you should feel honored to be one of the Lord's rejected messengers.

If you've been terminated for doing God's will, you need to hang on to two comforting truths: you're not alone, and He still has a plan for you. In fact, you've just joined thousands of colleagues who have also been run out of their churches for faithfully obeying God's call.

Even so, it's understandable to feel devastated and betrayed. To make matters even worse, the heartless bullies couldn't care less about how deeply they've hurt you. A terminated pastor describes how he felt:

> My family and I have been hurt deeply from having been run off from the church we loved and pastored for two-and-a-half years. As the deacons put it when I received the chilling news of my dismissal, "The last twenty years we have run off four preachers. We have already begun to pray that God will lead us to the right man to lead our church." It was as if a spike had been driven deep into my heart. I asked myself, *Did God know this was happening?*[71]

Thousands of ministers have endured this same harrowing experience. All wiped out and wondering what to do next. All unsure if they would ever recover, much less enter ministry again. If that describes you, please take a moment to drink from God's cup of encouragement. You can depend on His eternal love and involvement in your life now and forever.

Although it may appear that everything is completely out of control, if you will view your situation from God's standpoint, you will see that your *exit* from your bad situation is also an *entrance* into your new adventure. Rather than looking backward, turn your attention ahead of you. Instead of focusing on your past miseries, start preparing for future opportunities.

One terminated pastor, who was devastated by this abusive church, found out that God had a better plan for him:

> God is not finished with someone because of the mistakes of others. He used that situation to direct us to an alternative path that we hadn't planned. I liked to be in control of my destiny, but now everything was out of my hands and beyond my control. I had to learn to trust Him like never before. And God proved Himself to be faithful, and surprised me by opening doors that I wasn't expecting.

---

[71] J. B. Simmons, "Let's Run Off the Preacher" The Baptist Program.

God is fully aware of your desperate situation and has something very special planned for you. However, before you can move forward and receive His best, He must do something inside you to extricate the pain and heartache caused by the abuse you've received.

Let God Heal You
Typically, a wounded pastor finds his quickest relief by running as far from the abusive church as possible. So, he moves on to the next town, the next church, or the next state, hoping to leave all his troubles in the rearview mirror forever. However, when he gets to the next place, the ghosts of unresolved issues are waiting to haunt him.

For example, if a hothead named Bob gave him problems in his previous church, he can subconsciously become wary of every man he meets in the future with that name. Perhaps it's his looks, mannerisms, voice, or the way he laughs that dredges up the horrible memories of his former "Brutal Bob." Even fragrances like aftershave have a way of reminding him of past hurts.

Before you relocate to the next place, make sure that you've let go of all pastor abuse baggage. Have you forgiven and released those who persecuted you? Have you asked the Lord to heal your hurts? One of the most liberating measures you can take is to see your circumstances as completely in God's hands and under His control—in spite of how they look at the moment or what they've done to you.

If you've been terminated, your misfortune didn't take God by surprise, just like it didn't shock Him when Joseph's brothers threw him into a pit and sold him into slavery. Take note that you don't see Joseph angry and bitter at his brethren. Instead, he fully submitted himself to divine providence, knowing that God would actually use their hateful actions to fulfill His ultimate plan, which He did.

Shortly after Joseph was dumped into that underground dungeon in the wilderness, a group of Ishmaelite traders "just happened" to come along and purchase him. The spiteful brothers, who thought they had profited by disposing of their problem, were unknowingly filling in one of the pieces of the providential puzzle. God knew that a future famine was coming, and He needed a man in Egypt that He could trust to be a ruler. Transporting him to the new destination was an integral part in His plan.

Now let's think about that. If Joseph's brothers hadn't sold him into slavery, Joseph's promotion wouldn't have happened. He probably would have tended sheep until his dying day, and would not have fulfilled his destiny. But God, foreknowing that his jealous siblings would reject him, chose to use their rejection as His direction. Through His amazing sovereignty, He overruled their odious plot and orchestrated a magnificent plan to deliver Joseph into the right hands.

Looking past their hateful actions, we see God's hand actively at work. First, He guided the foreign traders along the correct path, at the perfect time to rescue him. If they had been just a few hours later or earlier, or even a mile off track, Joseph would have died in that pit.

However his brother, Judah, had come up with the idea of selling him to make a few quick bucks. (Could it be that God knew what they had planned and that suggestion was planted in Judah's noggin by the Lord Himself?) Precisely following the heavenly script, these merchants provided his transportation to Egypt, where they, without knowing it, "just happened" to deliver him to the divinely appointed address. There they sold him again, to the very person who "just happened" to have connections with the highest ruler in the land—Pharaoh. Joseph was eventually promoted to the second-highest position in Egypt.

Years later, Joseph was able to confidently declare what he knew to be true from the outset, "And as for you, *you meant evil against me, but God meant it for good* in order to bring about this present result . . ." (Gen. 50:20).

Pastor, as horrible as your pit may be or how abandoned you may feel, you have the opportunity to be like Joseph. The "brothers" who attacked you truly meant it for evil, but the Lord will use their intended mischief to get you to a new and better place, where He can bless you and your family for a long, long time. As Joseph's situation clearly demonstrates, man's rejection can be God's direction. Nothing is more therapeutic than to forgive your enemies, and to see His loving hand overruling their wicked actions.

God always has a prepared place for a prepared person. Just as God sent those traders along to relocate Joseph to a new place, He will send someone along to guide you to a better situation where He can use you more fully. However, it's imperative that you maintain a godly, trusting attitude and not develop a bitter "victim mentality." Your attitude will either lift you up to a promotion, or drag you down to destruction.

During this agonizing time when you're faced with making a life-changing decision, remember to trust God's wonderful promise: "And we know that God *causes all things to work together for good* to those who love God, to those who are called according to His purpose" (Rom. 8:28).

Pastor Mike Johnston shared his story of being abused in the first chapter. Here is what he has to say, years later:

> I've learned that the bitter tears we cry while being abused actually allows us to see fresh ministry amidst the *heaps of rubbish* left from the attack (Neh. 4:2). You may recall my story in chapter one about being run off from a church I loved and God was mightily blessing. Though I didn't know it at the time, the Lord was working His delightful purposes in me for greater ministry than I've ever known.
>
> I now devote much more time to Promise Ministries (PmiMinistries.com), an outreach I began to reach prisoners through evangelism and Bible college level Bible studies. To date 24,000 prisoners have been evangelized and or enrolled in our school.
>
> As you are evaluating the *walls and rubbish* left by the attacks on your life, please put it in a Proverbs perspective: "The godly may trip seven times, but they will get up again. But one disaster is enough to overthrow the wicked." (Prov. 24:16 NLT). Get up my friend! God's hand is upon you and your best ministry is just ahead.

My pastor-abuser experience was similar to what happened to Mike Johnston. My wife told me, "I can't take any more of this. We can find another church to attend, but please don't even consider being a pastor again."

I had been a man of integrity, worked hard to fulfill my responsibilities, and the church was growing. However, the small group of mean-spirited controllers made it impossible for me to keep ministering in that church. After I resigned, the abusers hired another pastor, and it wasn't long before they started unleashing hatred on him as well, trying to force him out. The abusive husband always beats up his next wife.

The good news is that after I left that church, God supernaturally opened a new door for me to work with a bestselling author. I helped him write a book for a Christian celebrity that is reaching many thousands of people. I also wrote the book you are now reading, which has helped pastors all over the United States and the world. God also opened a door for me to serve as an associate pastor in a much larger, loving congregation, which was like a breath of fresh air.

The Next Step

Most discarded ministers face double jeopardy when they try to find another job. Church search committees view them skeptically or worse, as damaged goods, because they were rejected by another congregation. And many secular employers see ministers as too specialized—unqualified for jobs that might provide comparable compensation. The money the pastor invested in his seminary education goes down the drain, as now he'll probably start over with a lower-paying job.

Nevertheless, the cold, hard facts of life dictate that we must work somewhere or we'll starve to death. Here are your four options:

Option #1 Look for another church to pastor.

Some shepherds immediately start hunting the next available pulpit, hoping that the new congregation will treat him better than the last one. However, such a place might be difficult to find, especially when you consider that many churches have vacant pastorates *for a reason*. Statistics show that one-third of pastors today serve in congregations where the previous pastor was forcefully terminated.[72]

The last thing you want to do is exchange a bad situation for another. One former pastor explained how he left his abusive church, only to accept an even worse situation:

> When I talked with the committee, they said, "We've interviewed a hundred men, and you're the man!" After several years of abuse, I left and interviewed with another church. That church told me, "You're exactly what we're looking for!" I bought that line again and accepted their call. They told me, "Just lead us, we're behind you." But when I turned around, they were after me with chain saws in their hands.

If you feel led to send out your resume, you would be wise to avoid those churches that have axed a pastor. Once they've run off one shepherd, it's much easier for them to do it the next time because they've set a precedent. Now they can mobilize their forces much faster when called upon.

One pastor interviewed with a church that had fired its previous shepherd. Wooed by the large salary, he foolishly ignored the warning

---

[72] Lori Arnold. "Ministry expands its outreach to terminated pastors" *Christian Examiner on the web*, July 2005, as quoted in www.christianexaminer.com/Articles/Articles%20Jul05/Art_Jul05_04.html.

signs and accepted their call. He soon discovered the congregation would abuse him just as they did his predecessor:

> My wife was uncomfortable when we visited the church for the first time. I was also uneasy after meeting some of the deacons, whom I suspected of being some of my predecessor's antagonists. Nevertheless, I was attracted by a larger salary and the prospect of a church in a fast-growing area. The church gave us a unanimous call. When the chairman of the deacons wanted an immediate answer, we accepted.
>
> Within minutes of our arrival home, a prestigious church called to say that I was at the top of their list of candidates. Within a week a larger church called with a serious inquiry. I wondered if I might have rushed into a decision that I would later regret. Time proved that my suspicions were correct. I lasted less than two years in that church.

Please understand that not all churches are abusive, so I don't want to frighten you out of ministry. There are many healthy, loving churches that treat their pastors well.

How can you distinguish a good church from a bad one? You can gather valuable information by simply calling the former pastors of the prospective churches. You can find out a lot of information by doing a little homework.

One fast, convenient place to find ministerial opportunities is on the Internet. You can select from hundreds of listings on sites such as www.churchstaffing.com, www.pastorfinder.com, www.simplyhired.com, www.ministersearch.com, www.churchstaffsearch.com, www.ministrysearch.com, www.churchjobs.net, and other sites that we have listed in the appendix.

While searching for a senior pastor opening, you might also want to consider an associate pastor position on a larger church's staff. There you can utilize your strengths, serve more effectively, and bring your experience alongside a man who really needs encouragement. Here are a few important questions to ask when searching for the next church:

- Does the church have a history of abusing and firing pastors?
- Does the church embrace the vision that God has planted in my heart?
- Are we in agreement over major points of theology?

- Are we on the same page whether the services will be traditional or contemporary?
- Does the church have a governmental structure that will allow me to lead?
- Are the current leaders in the church godly people?
- Is this church willing to let me lead them in the right direction, or will I have to change a lot of minds first?
- In the case of an associate pastor: Can I fully submit to the vision and leadership of the senior pastor?

Many of these questions can be answered by making a few phone calls and contacting the former pastors. The findings of this inquiry will determine whether you should continue to pursue the church or start looking for a different one.

Your best approach in tracking down a staff position is not to email your resume to every opening on the web, since fewer than one percent of job seekers actually get hired from responding to Internet job ads.[73] You're much more likely to get a positive response by targeting your resume to churches where you're a good fit. The one thing you don't want is to wind up in another abusive church, where they're set in their rigid ways and refuse to be led by God's Spirit.

Option #2 Plant a new church in a needy area.
Another option to prayerfully consider is starting a new church. This might be in the city where you live, a nearby town, or even a remote location in another state or country. Help is available from many sources, which offer everything from ministry and planning, to finances and building crews. However, the most important thing to remember when forming a new fellowship is that God must be in it.

Before you take a group with you from the abusive church to begin such a venture, ask yourself:

- Am I being led by the Holy Spirit or the spirit of revenge?
- Am I willing to commit myself for the long-haul, or will I pastor this new group only until a better opportunity arrives?

---

[73] Miller, Dan. *48 Days to the Work You Love*. Nashville: Broadman & Holman, 2005, 105.

- Are these people, who have left the former church, filled with anger, bitterness, and revenge; or do they genuinely desire to start a new church to glorify God and reach lost souls?
- Do I have a fellowship, association, or denomination that believes in this new church that will pray and offer assistance?
- Am I willing to work another job for as long as it takes?

Let's think through these extremely important questions.

First, don't submit to the spirit of revenge by pulling members out of your former church to pay back the abusers. If you do, you'll be joining the myriads of misdirected church pioneers who have sought to build a congregation merely from the ash heaps of termination, thinking their success will "get even." It won't work! Your motive is of the highest priority in God's eyes. If the Lord leads you to begin a new work, your efforts will be blessed in this endeavor. You must only plant a church if God's Spirit is leading you.

Second, you must commit yourself to shepherding this group for the long-haul. A word of extreme caution needs to be given; mission church planting is difficult and not a chore for the faint of heart. It can, and probably will, take years to establish ministries, find property, and construct a building. Are you willing to see this through?

I know from personal experience how difficult it is to plant a church from scratch. I was pastor of the church for eighteen years and worked a part-time job for much of the time. It took us many years to purchase land and construct a facility, and it only happened because the Lord gave us the strength to bring it to pass. My wife and I look back on that time of our lives with great satisfaction and fulfillment.

For the new work to be a success, it requires a godly vision and a burning passion. We've seen too many church plants start and fold due to lack of commitment from the pastor. Jesus warned short-range people about taking on long-term projects:

> "Suppose one of you wants to build a tower. What is the first thing you will do? Won't you sit down and figure out how much it will cost and if you have enough money to pay for it? Otherwise, you will start building the tower, but not be able to finish. Then everyone who sees what is happening will laugh at you" (Luke 14:28-29 CEV).

Although founding a new church is a challenging task, it's also an incredibly exciting adventure that can bring great reward. Count the cost, and if you're willing to pay the price, move forward.

Third, you'll never build a healthy, stable fellowship if the members are sick. A congregation composed of angry, bitter, and rebellious people will inevitably turn on its pastor. Even if a mass exodus of members has followed you out of the church, their attitude is more important than their numbers. Make sure that each former congregant who wants to be a part of the new church has forgiven the troublemakers who instigated your departure. If that root of bitterness is not uprooted, it will continue to grow until it produces bitter fruit again—in the new church!

Fourth, planting a church can get discouraging at times. If an established group endorses your new work, they can bring encouragement through counsel, prayer, and financial support. However, if no organization believes in what you're doing, it may mean you should look for other ways to fulfill your calling.

Finally, you may need to work another job for a while, until the church can pay you full-time. Statistics show that 35-40 percent of churches operate this way.[74] One church-planting pastor said, "My non-church job provided my insurance and most of my income, which allowed me to adequately provide for my family while the church was being established. When the congregation grew large enough, I went full-time with the church."

Option #3 Go back to school for training in a new field.

After spending several years studying in Bible School or seminary, you might find yourself feeling resentful when thinking about going back to school. But the fact is, earning another degree might be necessary for you to start a new career. Fortunately, you may be able to transfer some credits from the institutions you attended. You may consider a graduate degree in another field, or possibly enter a specialized field by attending a Vo-Tech school. A terminated pastor told us that went back to school to retool, and has had a fulfilling job as schoolteacher for a number of years.

---

[74] "Bivocational Ministry Emerging as Option." Kentucky Baptist Convention, November 5, 2002, as quoted in www.kybaptist.org.

Option #4 Find a secular job.

A current trend indicates that ministry is moving away from being carried out exclusively in established churches. Surveys conducted by Southern Baptists concluded that only one-third of their seminary graduates claim they intend to work in local church ministries.[75] In addition, a vast majority of students in other denominational seminaries are likewise avoiding church vocations. If this trend continues, we'll see less ministry taking place within the four cathedral walls and more in homes and in the marketplace.

Contrary to popular belief, if you resign from a church to work in a secular field, you have not "left the ministry." In some people's minds, the defining factor in determining whether a person is "in the ministry" is if he receives a church paycheck. Where is that in the Bible?

Changing from a church related job to one that is not is simply swapping vehicles in the way you share the gospel. Laboring at a secular job *is* ministry and therefore nothing to be ashamed of. In fact, you will find many of God's greatest servants in non-religious vocations including Abraham, Isaac, Jacob, Joseph, and Amos. Even the apostle Paul made tents while he preached and planted churches.

Your call to ministry is from God and has nothing to do with your earthly employer. Jesus said: "You did not choose Me, but I chose you and appointed you that you should go and bear fruit, and that your fruit should remain" (John 15:16 NKJV). This directive, which is meant for every disciple, compels us to serve the Lord in numerous ways—even outside of a church vocation and without a church paycheck.

You can teach Bible studies, Sunday school and discipleship classes, share the gospel, and visit the lonely, while enjoying some of the most fruitful ministry of your life. And don't forget that pastors are always looking for qualified candidates to fill the pulpit while they're away. And to think they tried to say you "left the ministry." (God knows better than that!)

Dan Miller, in his book *48 Days to the Work You Love*, writes:

> Nothing in Scripture depicts the Christian life as divided into sacred and secular parts. Rather, it shows a unified life, one of wholeness, in

---

[75] Wingfield, Mark. "Mentors in Ministry Matter: For the sake of the call." *The Baptist Standard*, October 2002, as quoted in www.baptiststandard.com/2002/10_7/pages/mentors.html.

which everything we do is service to God, including our daily work, whatever that may be.[76]

Martin Luther also believed that God equates secular labor on a par with ecclesiastical duties, if you're motive is to please the Lord. Several centuries ago he wrote: "The maid who sweeps her kitchen is doing the will of God just as much as the monk who prays. The Christian shoemaker does his Christian duty—not by putting little crosses on shoes, but by making good shoes, because God is interested in good craftsmanship."[77] He added, "The works of monks and priests, however holy and arduous they may be, do not differ one whit in the sight of God from the works of the rustic laborer in the field or the woman going about her household tasks, but that all works are measured before God by faith alone."[78]

Ex-pastors often feel like failures because they've been brainwashed into thinking they have left the ministry. While dejectedly endeavoring to make ends meet, they completely miss the incredible God-approved opportunity in their new assignment.

I stumbled upon another abused former pastor when I took my car to a local auto repair shop. Walter sat behind the desk, typing my information on the computer. During the course of our conversation, he casually mentioned that he "used to be in the ministry." This, of course, made me curious. After a moment of silence, I asked him what had happened.

Like many former pastors I know, Walt sensed God's call and enthusiastically enrolled in Bible College. There he studied vigorously; chomping at the bit to serve in a church, as he anxiously prepared for what he thought would be his lifelong vocation. After graduating, he ministered in three separate congregations in various staff positions—youth minister, administrative pastor, and minister of music. Now he wore mechanic's shirt and had stopped attending church.

"In each of my three churches, God was blessing my ministries," he explained. "New people were joining my programs and I was enjoying what I was doing. I really had a great relationship with most of the church members."

---

[76] Miller, 40.
[77] *Daily Bread.* Grand Rapids, MI: RBC Ministries, September 5, 1995.
[78] Miller, 41.

"Then what made you decide to quit working for a church?" I asked.

"In each church," he continued, "a small negative-minded group made my life miserable by constantly criticizing me over trivial issues. They could never see anything good I was doing, but only what they thought I was doing wrong. Their continual harassment just wore me out until I was so discouraged I couldn't take it anymore. It wore my wife out, too. More than once she had to bite her tongue while a church member lectured me about how to do ministry."

My heart could feel his pain as I envisioned exactly what he was talking about.

"The senior pastor was hassled even more than me," he admitted. "I finally realized that the church was killing us. I decided to get out of the ministry so I could protect my wife and preserve my mental health. Thankfully, my father owns several car repair shops, so I was able to take over this one."

I've talked with Walt several times since this first meeting. He's started attending church again and is enjoying his job. And because he meets new people every day, he now has a wide-open door of ministry that he didn't have before.

Job Considerations

If you've been terminated, the question you're probably asking yourself is *where can I find a job to support my family?* Although Walt was blessed to have a secular job waiting for him, most pastors who are forced out have nowhere to turn. They've spent years serving in churches and a different career field would require them to go back to college. If God doesn't open up a door quickly, they could find themselves standing on the streets holding up a cardboard sign that reads: "Will Translate Greek for Food."

Despite the process, making the switch—from working in the church to working in the world—can actually become an exciting adventure. We have found that many former pastors find their new professions both fulfilling and liberating. Some are, quite honestly, giddy about not having to put up with troublesome church members anymore. They are actually more effective in their ministries because they're no longer tied to unrealistic demands connected with a church paycheck.

A former pastor explained one advantage he discovered: "I can now share the gospel with others without them questioning my motives. When I was a pastor, they often viewed my witnessing for Christ as part of my paid job. Now that I am supported by other means, the impact has seemingly become much greater."

If you've been involved in church related ministry most of your life, you know that church politics and petty issues can sidetrack you from the things that really matter. A secular job may be just the thing to rejuvenate your spiritual life.

What secular jobs should you be looking for, and what are you qualified for? The answer is found in your *transferable skills*. When you really think about it, your experience in the pastorate has actually equipped you very well for a number of occupations.

We suggest that you conduct a self-examination and write down your skills, which can be readily transferred to an employer who needs them. You can begin by searching online newspapers and websites such as www.intercristo.com. You can also investigate www.hotjobs.com and www.monster.com to find openings.

Here are some suggestions for specific types of jobs:

- **Management.** If you love overseeing people, apply for management positions in department stores, restaurants, nursing homes, car rental companies, or other businesses with numerous employees. Christian bookstore chains such as Lifeway Stores and Family Christian Stores are continually looking for honest, industrious store managers. Your resume should focus on your skills rather than your employment locations.
- **Motivational speaking.** If you're a good communicator, you'll probably have success in sales or advertising. You might consider starting your own business using your speaking abilities, and you can certainly find some work as a pulpit supply or interim pastor.
- **Denominational Vocations.** You may be well-qualified for a position with your denomination and still guest preach in various churches on weekends.
- **Mercy/Compassion/Visitation.** Consider being a chaplain in a nursing home or hospital. These are two prime areas that need a compassionate person to minister to those searching for hope. Funeral homes are often in need of ministers to conduct memorial services. The transition should be relatively easy in these cases.

- **Chaplaincy/Evangelism.** Besides nursing homes and hospitals, look at the possibilities of being a chaplain in prisons, police and fire departments, colleges, and the military. Volunteer to preach or teach Bible studies at jails and prisons where over two million inmates currently reside. That's a mission field white unto harvest!
- **Parachurch Ministry.** Search the Internet for "parachurch ministry jobs" and you'll find openings that might be a perfect fit. They may be looking for a person with your experience.
- **Real Estate.** Many former pastors have become real estate agents and have done very well in this profession.
- **Home Improvements.** You might consider starting a home improvement business if you have skills in carpentry, electrical, plumbing, painting, roofing, hanging sheetrock, interior decorating, or lawn care.
- **Author/Publisher.** Your years of experience as a pastor can be a goldmine for a less seasoned minister. To be quite honest, only a select few can make a career from writing books and articles for Christian periodicals. However, it's easier to get an article published in a magazine than to receive a book contract, and you have the experience to write that piece. If it gets published, you can reach as many as 100,000 people or more with your advice. To get started, you need to attend a Christian writers conference in your area, which will instruct you how to proceed. Visit www.stuartmarket.com for more information. Although you probably can't support your family through writing, it can be a way to minister to people.
- **Teacher/Professor.** Many bi-vocational pastors have paid their own salaries by teaching in public or Christian schools throughout their ministry career. Even if you don't want to be a full-time schoolteacher, you can find temporary work by becoming a substitute teacher in the school system. You can even specify which grades you're willing to teach. If you have a Master's degree, consider applying with colleges and universities that are looking for instructors to teach Bible or religion-related courses.
- **Fundraising.** If you are effective in asking people for money, you have an abundance of opportunities available. Many colleges, both Christian and secular, are searching for Development

officers, who will visit alumni, businessmen, and others to request funds for their respective schools. Once you've gained some experience in this field, other organizations will want to hire you, and some will offer six-figure salaries.

- **Languages.** If you can fluently speak another language, many businesses will be quick to hire you. Our society has become a melting pot of many languages, and businesses realize the value of bilingual employees.
- **Delivery Companies.** United Parcel Service, FedEx, the United States Post Office, and other delivery businesses often hire new people and pay very good wages.
- **Government Jobs.** Look into civil service, city, county, state, and federal job openings.
- **Colleges and Universities**. Search the Internet for job openings at colleges and universities.
- **Insurance companies.** Insurances companies are always looking for highly motivated individuals for sales and other positions. Being an insurance adjuster can produce a decent income for your family, and doesn't take years of training.
- **Sales.** Someone once said, "Nothing happens until someone sells something." One roadblock to sales success is an inbred fear of speaking in front of people. You have made your living doing this. Consider retail businesses, automobile sales, and real estate. Your ability to sell what you believe is needed on many fronts and often can provide you with a very comfortable living and many opportunities to share your faith in Jesus.
- **Technical**. If you have computer skills, website experience, or are knowledgeable about musical and sound equipment, highlight your expertise on your resume.
- **Start your own business.** One ex-pastor, who had to provide for his wife and 5 children, loved to paint faux finishes on the walls of elegant homes, using sponges, rags, and brushes. He's now making 8 to 10 times the income he was generating previously, and is able to minister to many people outside of the church.[79]

---

[79] Miller.

- **Other.** Don't discount anything. Consider being a radio disc jockey. If you like to drive trucks, remember that God can use Christian truck drivers. If you enjoy construction, don't dismiss your passion, but fulfill it by looking for construction work.
- **Network through your contacts.** If none of the above are applicable, start thinking about who you know. Your contacts might be the best place to begin in finding work. Let them know that you're looking for work and if they know of anything available to contact you.

Remember dear brother, that God loves you, has chosen you, and *does* have a plan for you! This passage, written by Solomon three thousand years ago, still applies today: "Trust in the Lord with all your heart, and lean not unto your own understanding. In all your ways acknowledge Him, and *He shall direct your paths*" (Prov. 3:5-6 NKJV).

Appendix

A Pastor's Wife Speaks Out

I interviewed a terminated pastor's wife, who served with her husband in churches for twenty-five years. Even though her husband had successfully grown two congregations, he was cruelly mistreated in each church. In both situations, he was forced out by a small group of members who angrily resisted change. The former pastor and his wife now serve the Lord in evangelical ministries.

Were you prepared for the conflict you experienced during your ministry?
Ministers go to school to learn how to do ministry. But women who marry ministers usually go to college to be a nurse or teacher. So we marry into a profession that we were not trained to do.

And even when my husband studied for ministry, he never took a class called "Dealing with Elders 101." They never trained him for the conflict he would face. So he went into the ministry unprepared for battles that he would encounter, and I'm not trained at all of being able to handle that. And that's why many ministers' wives will say, "You know, I really didn't ask for this and here I am in the middle of it! I don't want to do this."

When you get into these tough situations, where your husband is about to be terminated for no good reason, it's more personal than just being fired from any job. That ministry has pulled you into the conflict, and you're getting fired too. And you didn't even ask to be hired!

What went through your mind when your husband was terminated?
When he was fired, I was shocked. It had just been a week before that he had received a glowing report on his evaluation. The church was really doing well—it was growing and the spirit was good. The church had grown during the summertime when churches normally don't grow.

The elder had come to my husband on Christmas Eve and told him he needed to resign that coming Sunday. The entire church was in shock because we couldn't tell anyone he was resigning or why. The elders told us we couldn't say anything about it or they would stop giving the severance pay. So we resigned and left town, without being able to give an explanation.

What was the hardest part for you?
The hardest thing was watching my husband being accused of things he wasn't guilty of. Watching people be unfair. Watching people mistreat our children. It's hard to sit back and be quiet, and see those things happen—especially to hear all the lies.

It really hurts when the elders do not back your husband when he's being attacked, or when they are saying one thing and doing another. It hurts when you see your friends, or people you thought were your friends, turning against you, simply because they're afraid of trying something new and different.

However, the minute we left the church was the biggest relief in the world. I had watched my husband grieve over the conflict in the church. But we really didn't have a ministry in that church. We were just babysitting a bunch of people who wanted to misbehave and throw fits, and it was nice to get away from that.

Are you happy with your new ministry, which isn't in a church?
We stuck it out long enough, and felt free when we left the pastorate. When my husband was a pastor, all of our time, energy, and resources were being consumed with things that made absolutely no difference in the kingdom. So we asked ourselves why on earth do we want to spend our lives that way?

If you could see how much he is doing in the way of ministry now, compared to how our hands were tied when we were in a congregation, and how happy he is now compared to then—why would I ever want him to go back that?

I wouldn't trade where we are now. My husband is happier than he's ever been. He serves in a parachurch ministry where he's able to help other ministers and churches. I'm also working for an evangelical ministry, so we're out doing good things and not having to deal with petty issues anymore. It's a relief!

Since we've left, several churches have called my husband to see if he would consider being their pastor. I give him the look: *don't even go there!* He's really happy and fulfilled with what he's doing now, so why should we go back?

Don't get me wrong; not everything was bad about being a minister's wife. We made many good friends and accomplished some good things. In every situation, we had elders who loved and supported us. We had very supportive and encouraging church members. We still have many great friends in those churches.

But I don't want to go back there because of what it evolved to, and we don't have much time left before our lives on earth will be over. We'll only have one or two short ministries left in us, so how do we want to spend it? We chose to spend our remaining years serving in ministries that we love and are making a difference. We're serving the Lord and not having to deal with pettiness.

Although I never complained about my role, after we left the church I told my husband, "I just love not having to be a pastor's wife!" I don't have to play a part anymore or feel guilty about not meeting everyone's expectations. I used to have to go to everything going on at the church, but now I can choose what I want to do. I just get to be a Christian now.

The Fellowship of His Sufferings

Can you imagine how Jesus must have felt as He walked in total obedience to His Father, yet was constantly hated and slandered throughout His ministry? And His greatest resistance came from the most respected religious leaders of that day—the Pharisees. Only He and His Father in heaven understood the sufferings that He experienced.

The apostle Paul tells us that we can gain a new level of understanding through "the fellowship of His sufferings" (Phil. 3:10). No one in their right mind goes searching for ways to experience pain. No one *wants* to suffer. In fact, we usually avoid it at all costs. Yet, as we seek to know God in a more intimate way, the forces of hell are unleashed upon us through antagonistic individuals.

Peter tells us, "For you have been called for this purpose, since Christ also suffered for you, leaving you an example for you to follow in His steps (1 Pet. 2:21). As you follow His steps, as things get tougher you will find that you're walking alone. It's on this lonely road of suffering that you will learn more about God than at any other time in your life.

You can't learn "the fellowship of His suffering" through studying books. You'll only learn this level of anguish when it is thrust upon you. The following ten things happened to Jesus and to some degree will also happen to you. When it does, don't be alarmed. You are entering into a new depth of your walk with Christ.

To enter into "the fellowship of His sufferings" the following must take place:

1. You must be blameless; a person of integrity.
2. Your greatest ambition is to love and please the Lord at all costs.
3. You will be rejected by a group of modern-day Pharisees or Sadducees, who act religiously but resist everything that God wants to do through you.
4. The Pharisees and Sadducees will meet secretly to plot your demise.

5. Even though you are innocent, you will be slandered and gossip will be spread about you in your community.
6. A close friend whom you trust will betray you.
7. When you're being attacked, your supporters will back away and will not come to your defense.
8. You and the Lord will be the only ones who understand that you're innocently suffering.
9. You will go through a "crucifixion" experience—harassed, abused, and possibly terminated from your job or ousted from your church.
10. God will resurrect you with a better and more powerful ministry. Paul describes this as the "power of His resurrection" (Phil. 3:10).

Bad Resume
(Guaranteed to keep you from being hired)

Name: Ben Booted
14365 Mourning Ave.
Whineville, Texas

Height: 5'4"
Weight: 355 lbs.
Health: Dangerously high blood pressure, emphysema.

Education:
Middle School: Bright Minds Middle School, spilling bee champion
High School: Benedict Arnold High School, 1999, v.p. of stamp club
College: Generic Bible College, 2003, 2.6 GPA
Seminary: N.E.B.T.S., M.R.E., 2008 (Worked for Harry's Pizza while attending seminary, took 5 years to graduate)

Secular Experience:
- Deliveryman for Harry's Hand-Tossed Pizza. Set record for most pizzas delivered in an hour.
- Installed chain link fence for Links & More Fence Company.

Ministry Experience:
2011-Present
Pastor, Abusive Baptist Church, Whineville, Texas
- Did same things as in previous church (see below)
Reason for leaving: Was run off by Justa Meandeacon and Ima Busybody.

2008-2011
Pastor, Niceville Baptist Church, Pleasant Town, Virginia
- Responsible for preaching
- Visited sick folks
- Responsible for planning services

- Responsible for conducting funerals and weddings
- Planned church dinners (pot lucks and stuff)
  Reason for leaving: I felt led to accept the wonderful salary package offered by Justa Meandeacon at Abusive Baptist Church.

References:
>
> Ima Busybody
> 425 Slander Street
> Whineville, Texas
> 555-1212
>
> Justa Meandeacon
> 666 Control Court
> Whineville, Texas
> 555-0666
>
> The Rev. Billy Graham
> Minneapolis, Minnesota

The purpose of a resume

Would you hire the person based on the above resume? The *only* purpose of a resume is to get you an interview. God does expect you to knock on doors. Your responsibility is to put together an excellent, well-written resume and send it to targeted churches. God's responsibility is to open the correct door for you.

The pastor search committee at Greener Pastures Church is sorting through two hundred resumes and can only choose one person. Their responsibility is to prayerfully search for and connect with the right candidate. Your resume is the only piece of information they have to evaluate you. With that in mind, tell them what God has gifted you to do and honestly state your accomplishments.

Let's consider what's wrong with the above resume:

Health:

Your resume isn't a medical report so why mention your health?

Education:
No need to mention middle school or high school. Make sure that you have corrected your typographical errors. The search committee doesn't care if you were the "spilling" bee champion or the stamp club VP. It might even send the opposite message—that you are desperately grasping for accomplishments to impress them. Don't mention your GPA and be sure to spell out the name of your seminary.

Secular Experience:
Exclude part-time jobs if possible. Unless your secular experience can enhance your ministry, it probably won't mean much to those reviewing your resume. Your abilities in technology, music, teaching, writing, and management should be noted, especially if you lack ministry experience.

Ministry Experience:
This is the most important part of your resume. Committees want to know exactly what you did to grow and strengthen your previous churches. They already know that you're responsible for preaching, visiting the sick, planning services, and conducting funerals and weddings. You're not writing a job description, so don't write down what you're "responsible for."

What were some of your accomplishments?

Did you establish an outreach program or some other valid ministry?

How many people were saved and baptized?

Can you give specific examples of lives that were changed?

Did you lead a building program?

Did Sunday school enrollment increase?

Did you write articles for Christian magazines?

All these achievements give the committee an idea of your track record and what they might expect from you.

References:
Who in their right mind would list someone who doesn't like you? You need to include supporters in your current and previous churches who will give you a glowing recommendation. Be sure to ask your references' permission before you list them. If they receive a phone call from the search committee, they don't need to be caught off-guard.

And just because you shook Billy Graham's hand doesn't make him a reference. Avoid including famous people that you barely know. It would be embarrassing if they called about you, and he or she says, "Who?" However, if well-known person is actually willing to endorse you, go ahead and include his or her name. You can also add "additional references available upon request."

Good Resume

Ben Hired
1000 Wonder Lane
Happy, Texas
555-7777

Objective
To serve as senior pastor in a contemporary evangelical church, equipping Christians for the work of ministry.

Education
    Seminary: Northern Evangelical Bible Theological Seminary
            Masters of Religious Education, 2008.
    College: Generic Bible College
            Bachelor of Arts in Theology, 2003.
            Recipient of the President's Achievement Award for Outstanding Student.

Ministry Experience
2011-Present
    Pastor, Harmony Baptist Church, Happy, Texas
- Established an evangelism and outreach program.
- Won 47 to Christ and baptized 39 in last year.
- Increased Sunday school enrollment by 35%.
- Grew morning worship average attendance from 175 to 250.
- Raised $395,000 and led church construction for the new education wing.

2008-2011
    Pastor, Niceville Baptist Church, Pleasant Town, Virginia
- Grew average morning worship attendance from 85 to 190.
- Increased Sunday school enrollment 40%.
- Hired and managed paid and volunteer staff of 8.
- Implemented a Children's Church program during the worship service.

- Led in the construction of a $200,000 addition to the sanctuary.
- Published an article entitled "Ministering to the Divorced" in *Discipleship Weekly*.

Skills

Preaching: Preached revivals in Texas, Georgia, and Oklahoma.

Computer: Proficient using variety of church computer programs. Designed church website.

Music: Play guitar. Lead music.

References

Heeza Goodman (deacon, Harmony Baptist Church)
531 Graceland Drive
Happy, Texas
555-9404

Gladys Sweet (member, Niceville Baptist Church)
777 Nectar Lane
Pleasant Town, Virginia
555-7685

Internet Job Listings

Here are some websites that list openings for ministry and non-ministry employment. All links were active at the time this publication. Carefully read everything on these websites before agreeing to or signing anything.

Ministry Employment
www.jobleads.org
www.churchcentral.com
www.churchjobs.net
www.christianet.com/christianjobs
www.christianitytoday.com/career
www.churchstaffing.com
www.churchstaffsearch.com
www.denverseminary.edu/job-board
www.familychristian.com
www.theshepherdsstaff.com
www.lifeway.com
www.ministrysearch.com
www.ministersearch.com
www.ministerconnection.net
www.resume.monster.com
www.youthspecialties.com/jobbank
www.onlinechristianmall.com/jobs
www.christiansunite.com/classifieds
www.gospelcom.net/ccc/jobs
www.christianjobs.com
www.youthpastor.com/jobs
www.pastorsearch.net
www.jobseekers.org
www.spiritrestoration.org/Pastor_jobs_Church_openings.htm
www.garbc.org/pastorsearch.php
www.mbcpathway.com/classifieds
www.ministryemployment.com
www.ministryjobs.com
www.christianjobs.com
www.intercristo.com
m77staffing.com/job-postings

Secular Employment
www.monster.com
www.careers.org
www.intercristo.com
www.hotjobs.yahoo.com
www.jobsniper.com
www.careerbuilder.com
www.careers.msn.com
www.jobweb.com
www.job.com
www.jobfind.com
www.jobhuntersbible.com
www.jobsearch.org
www.lawenforcementjobs.com
www.hospitaljobsonline.com
www.dice.com
www.jobster.com
www.ajb.dni.us
www.nationjob.com
www.business.com
www.nurse-recruiter.com
www.officer.com
www.snagajob.com
www.pavisnet.com/jobs (Focused on the Northeastern Job Market)

You can also search the Help Wanted ads in newspapers, many of which can be accessed online.

Online Job Directories (listing several employment sites)
- Environmental careers www.webdirectory.com/Employment
- Google Directory www.google.com/Top/Business/Employment

Helpful Resources (Information is copied from the respective websites)
- **Contract Job Hunter** www.cjhunter.com
  ContractJobHunter.com is a product of C.E. Publications. Contract Employment Weekly, our print publication, has been

keeping contract job seekers informed about contract opportunities in the Design, Engineering, IT/IS, and Technical disciplines for over 37 years. Whether you're a technical professional searching for contract employment or a recruiter seeking to fill an open contract job, we can help you make your next connection.

- **Employment Guide** www.employmentguide.com
  EmploymentGuide.com is the leading job board for hourly, skilled, full-time and part-time jobs. Since its inception in 1995, the EmploymentGuide.com job board has provided an optimum combination of hiring solutions and job search options across numerous job industries nationwide. Our focus is on part time jobs online and entry-level to mid-management employment opportunities.
- **All Freelance** www.allfreelance.com
  Freelance Jobs Directory offers self-employed small business owners links to freelance & work at home job boards, self-promotion tips, contract employment, lists of self-employment health/medical insurance for freelancers, jobs for freelance graphic designers, web designers, artists, illustrators, and other self-employed home-based small business professionals.

How to Order More Copies of This Book

www.kentcrockett.com

Online orders: www.kentcrockett.com

Check or Money Order:
Send a check or money order made out to "Kent Crockett."

The prices below include shipping and handling to one address in the United States. Books will be shipped Media Mail.
For orders to be shipped outside of the United States, a minimum order of 2 books is required due to mailing costs.

Single copy	$15
2 copies	$27
3 copies	$38
4 copies	$46
5 copies	$55
6 or more	$10 per book

Mail to: Kent Crockett
125 E. Poplar St.
Prattville, Alabama 36066

If you have questions about ordering, you can email me at kent@kentcrockett.com.

Kent Crockett websites

www.kentcrockett.com   Free sermon illustrations for pastors.

www.kentcrockett.blogspot.com   Sign up for Kent's free weekly devotionals sent by email.

www.makinglifecount.net   The official ministry website of Kent Crockett. Hundreds of free printable Bible studies and other resources.

Follow Kent on Twitter: @KentCrockett

Books by Kent Crockett

Slaying Your Giants

Filled with inspiring stories, thought-provoking insights, and heart-warming humor, *Slaying Your Giants* gives biblical step-by-step methods to help you defeat 20 invisible giants you will face in life. An additional Study Guide is available for small group studies.

The Sure Cure for Worry

Do you feel hopeless about your future? Are you terrified that an economic collapse or some other tragedy will occur? The Sure Cure for Worry gives proof that you can trust God to guide and provide for you, even when the world appears to be out of control.